Chi
A Journey With Me!

How to Reach Wholeness

Lesley Ford

outskirts
press

TABLE OF CONTENTS

ACKNOWLEDGMENTS

SINCERE THANKS TO my handsome husband and friend for understanding my need to retreat and go into my writing zone throughout the years. I've been journaling for as long as we've been married and he has always been so supportive of my alone time. He accepts and loves me just the way I am and for that I am grateful. Thank you baby! I Love you so much!

Thank you to my grandparents for teaching me how to live life on my own terms. Even though my grandmother birthed thirteen babies, she never pressured me to get pregnant. She understood that I was in control of my body and my decision to forego motherhood was mine to make. I learn so much by being in my grandparents' presence. Listening to their stories and laughing about any and everything is so comforting to me. I have a connection with my grandmother that will be with me for the rest of my days. I am definitely Irene's grandchild!

I have to thank my parents for loving me unconditionally and being my prayer warriors. They have supported me with so many dreams and nightmares, I can't even begin. They are my motivators! They are my heroes! I love, love, love you!

To my siblings who are all so unique and full of love. Thank you for putting up with me and loving me, even when I may have been unlovable (which I can't think of an example, but....LOL). I love you each so much it makes my heart hurt!

To all my extended family, and Lord knows there's about 1,100 of you. I love us......from the Cutrights to the Dawsons, the Fords, Williams, Robinsons, Thompsons, Lakeys, Huckabys, and Mannings...I love you all.

To the friends I've had for 25+ years and friends I met recently, you are queens! Thank you for all the laughs, tears, talks, and especially for all the memories. I keep my inner circle small but my love for you is big. I love each of you in a special way.

To all the students that I had the pleasure of meeting, you have no idea how much I learned from you and how you influenced and touched my life. Thank you! I hope you are somewhere out there shining your light!

Last but absolutely not least, thank you God for choosing me. Thank you for my life. Thank you for blessing me so I can bless others.

FOREWORD

HAVING IT ALL! What exactly does it mean? Why do we use this phrase for what life is supposed to look like? Is it even realistic to have it all? Who has it all and what exactly do they have? Is it the perfect family? Perfect house? Perfect bank account? Perfect body? Who says having these things make for a perfect life? This fairytale created by American society is not only false but has created a mindset that has been setting us up for failure for far too long. Sometimes just the way we think about a situation can make all the difference. I believe that goes for life as well. Instead of trying to have it all or have what some call a "perfect" life, the American dream, why can't we celebrate doing life well? We have so many standards and expectations in life that are all for nothing if we don't understand how to live well. Peace, joy, love, compassion, and a willingness to do for others are values that were left out of America's dream.

I chose to be a child-free woman but that doesn't mean I'm freed from the responsibility to help nurture, guide, and enlighten all children. Adults have a responsibility to children, not the other way around. In a country where we like to take credit for being child-centered, our actions show otherwise. To profess one thing and refuse to actually make it a priority is a contradiction more people in this country should be outraged about.

We don't need to have it all, we need to ensure that ALL have.

According to most U.S. census data, having six to nine children was common for women in the 1900s. Women had different reasons, of course, for having many kids. Some of those reasons included: lack of birth control, wanting to ensure parents were taken care of in their old age, longer child-bearing years, children being viewed as assets, and a lack of "outside of the home" work for women. In addition, the culture dictated that a woman's place was in the home, and her fulfillment was found there, where she served her husband and raised their children.

In his 1983 book *Family and Divorce in California, 1850-1890*, University of Oklahoma historian Robert Griswold cited an article published in the San Mateo Gazette in the mid-19th century that states, "Woman is set in the household and man is sent out into the world." Even a woman of modest means could "be happy in the love of her husband, her home, and its beautiful duties without asking the world for its smiles and favors," the article argued.

Unfortunately, not much has changed. This pathology was and still is the "American dream" for many. As long as you have a man providing for you, you can focus on household duties and having babies while allowing your husband to fill up your love tank and make you whole. What a gentleman, right? Not quite, more like what a burden! No human being can make you whole nor is it their responsibility to do so. We are all responsible for our own wholeness, whether married or single.

My reason for writing this book is not to bash men nor diminish the value of a good man. My goal has always been to empower women. Women like myself who have chosen to not become mothers and still desire a full and complete life. My "why" is to give another perspective to life when you step outside of the "typical" standards and expectations. To encourage the upcoming generations to choose wisely, be intentional about their lives, purpose and gifts. Start inward with loving yourself before looking outward for love. My hope is to shift the conversations and expectations we have regarding girls and women, while offering everyday strategies, along with my experiences, to help you live your BEST LIFE!

Fast forward to more current data, it is said that approximately 1 out of 7 adult women do not have children. Unlike the days when women relied on men, the younger generations are deciding to forego parenthood because of financial reasons, climate/global control, and of course the many pandemics we are facing today. A lot of people are more focused on contributing on a collective level rather than a more personal level. One thing I do know is that our decision to be child-free is not even a drop in the bucket towards human extinction, so please don't be fearful of that.

These days not only do women fill up our own "tanks," we drive our own vehicles and take the roads less traveled for real adventure. When planning a trip, some automatically think of booking the first flight out, while others map out the most scenic route to their destination. Still, a few may find the best all-inclusive staycation for a hassle-free, close to home getaway for day or two. My husband and I love to travel and get lost, away from it all. We enjoy mixing it up. Whether we're jumping on a flight or packing our car for a road trip, we are here for it. But for us, it does not include cruises. We tried a short 3-day cruise and had a great time with our friends but ultimately, my husband is not a fan! His thing is, how can you explore and get lost when everything and everyone is right there? He feels a bit claustrophobic and dirty, lol! I'm amazed that I even talked him into trying it out. On the contrary, my siblings and their spouses love a long seven-day cruise, popping in and out of various exotic locations and being amongst tourists and locals from all over the world. So even though we all love to vacation, the type of getaway deemed enjoyable and relaxing differs depending on who you ask. That's exactly how I view life in general. The type of lifestyle deemed enjoyable depends on who you ask. There is no longer a one size fits all model.

While writing my story, it seemed as though the analogy of travel kept coming up, so I just went with it. After all, this is my journey, my truth, and I choose to take the path less traveled. I hope my journey fuels your journey and allows you to think outside the box! Being able to make your own way and having faith that your journey can and will bring fulfillment is so empowering. We are not meant to live sad, depressed, anxiety-filled lives. Whatever path you have chosen for your journey, if you are breathing then your life is to be celebrated and lived in abundance. Whether your path looks like the majority of Americans or not, it is yours to enjoy. This idea of the American dream is a fictional myth that was never really a dream for most people. Our purpose is not to fit in and be like everyone else. The American dream was built off of the blood, sweat, and tears of marginalized people, who wants that dream? Even though we are aware of this truth, we continue to perpetuate this romanticized narrative that there is only one way to be happy. Maybe that's why our society is so broken. Maybe that's why America has so much depression and anxiety despite being the wealthiest country. Perhaps, we have lost ourselves trying to fit into a dream that is a figment of our imagination. We are so quick to characterize something as wrong or less than to justify what we want to be right. America is great at promoting values and beliefs that only benefit a certain demographic.

This fictitious dream can no longer serve as our life aspiration. Chasing that dream will leave us distressed and empty. We have misconstrued the real purpose in life since the conception of this country. The ultimate dream should be to love one another, bless others, and be of service, plain and simple. We are meant to live full and meaningful lives regardless of what it "looks" like. This is a new day and we should be viewing the world with new lenses. America's infectious wounds do not require band-aids, they need exposure to heal. Conversations provide recourse for remedy. Let's start talking candidly so we can LIVE OUR BEST LIFE!

There are many ways to achieve the gratifying life you so deserve. Child-free living or "CF Life" is an option to assumed mother/fatherhood, which is often portrayed as the only way to happiness. Many women of a certain age, single, and no children, almost always view themselves as a failure or not enough to some degree. In my opinion, a lot of this negative thinking comes from years and years of advertising the "American dream" to manipulate that mentality. In no way am I implying that people should not marry or reproduce, only giving another perspective of what a desirable life can also consist of. Be bold, be informed, and embrace who you truly are. It has been made very clear that we no longer need permission to create new normals. By the end of this book, readers will know how to find genuine fulfillment even if they choose to forego motherhood, never get married or live up to the copious amount of expectations society deems acceptable.

A full life with passion and purpose is within your reach, keep reading and keep driving! Oh and don't forget to turn up the music!

Speaking of music, it has always been a refuge. Music speaks to my soul and ministers to my spirit. I fell in love with music as a young girl riding in the back of my mom's blue Datsun, singing along to the soulful voices of Gladys Knight and the Pips, Patti, Stephanie Mills, Teddy Pendergrass, Stevie Wonder and so many more. Groups like DeBarge, The Jets, and New Edition still make me reminisce when I hear them. I used to love harmonizing with my sister as we sang backup for Diana Ross, I mean my aunt, while we were driving around town in her beautiful sports car. You couldn't tell us nothin'!

Growing up in the church, I also had a very instinctive relationship with gospel greats like Mahalia Jackson, Shirley Caesar, The Hawkins, The Winans, and The Clark Sisters, to name a few. Gospel music is always my go to.

Music also became a part of my DNA growing up during the time when The original and undeniable best rap and hip hop music of all time, was created. I was fortunate to have witnessed the most talented musicians transform everyday life into a cultural phenomenon. It gave people who looked like me a new angle to vocalize and reveal the injustices that were (are) ever so present. The mixture of all those genres is what flows through my veins today. Nowadays everyone thinks they know hip-hop—as a matter of fact, the kids today really believe they ARE hip-hop, bless their hearts! When I reflect on what hip-hop truly was, I think of artists such as the Sugar Hill Gang, Kool Moe Dee, Whodini, Public Enemy, Heavy D, Queen Latifah, MC Lyte, LL Cool J, Ice Cube, E40, Yo-yo, Tupac and this list goes on.

So, it is quite natural for music to be representative of the different stages and seasons throughout my journey. I have included a song title and artist at the beginning of each chapter that spoke to me as I was writing. I also remember, back in the day, when having a dope soundtrack to accompany a movie was just as important as the movie itself. Music has always been in my blood so infusing it somehow in my writing was a must! I hope you enjoy my playlist. When I'm journaling and reflecting, songs will come to mind that I can't seem to stop singing. Sometimes it's for a moment and other songs I will sing for days on end. When I'm sad, I sing. When I'm happy, I sing. When I'm praying, I sing. When I'm working, I sing. And of course, when I'm driving, I sing my best. So it was only fitting to have my own soundtrack to enhance and compliment my story, my journey. Buckle up and Enjoy!

Step 1

RENEWING YOUR MIND

SONG
"CLOSER"
GOAPELE

DID YOU GROW up dreaming about one day becoming a mom? As a young girl, did you fantasize about your wedding day? Did your mom discuss with you how she couldn't wait for you to become a mother or make her a grandmother? Were you told that you had to get married by a certain age and become a mommy? Were you told that you had to "give" your husband babies? Was it implied that there was only one way to achieve a happy life?

Well most girls, no matter the country or culture

you were born into, were shown their role in life. Whether it was directly told to us or subtly depicted for us, we got the message! Girls become moms and do whatever it takes to make a beautiful home for their spouse and family. You know the visual: married by a certain age to your knight in shining armor, at least 2.5 kids (whatever that meant), white picket fence and a dog. We've allowed this to be the goal for many, many decades.

I don't think this is wrong necessarily, it's just a decision that should be made individually. But before making a lifelong decision, it is so crucial to take some time to think about your "why." Do you feel pressured? Are you comparing? Do you feel as though you do not have other options? Getting married by a certain age and having babies as soon as you get married is so domineering. To minimize females to their anatomy alone is no different than sexual exploitation. This limits women to sexual objects without regard to the implications it may have. Yes, our bodies are capable of many things and giving birth is absolutely the most mind-blowing and exalted of them all. This important feat should not be taken lightly. Before grooming girls to be wives and mothers, she needs to understand her body, how sacred and miraculous it is. She has to develop her identity, her voice and be shown how to face challenges with grace. These may be hard conversations to have but they are so necessary. We can't just jump into dating or being a mommy without teaching girls to be cognizant of who they are. Helping our young girls navigate through social, emotional, and spiritual awareness must come first. This awareness starts with our thinking, renewing our mind. As young girls we are encouraged to be nurturers. I do believe it is part instinct, but I also believe it is taught. Women have a long history of taking care of or nurturing everyone except themselves. This begins when we are children. Young girls have not been taught to put themselves first. We take care of things/people. Unfortunately, we subconsciously put the pressure of having babies on our girls way too often and much too soon. Think about it, little girls are told their dolls are their babies or their younger siblings are their babies. I know we've all heard it and usually think it's cute. These are subliminal messages that do not serve the child. Why does a four year old little girl need to be told she has a baby? If it's a sibling, say brother or sister, rather than her baby. If it's a toy, by all means call it a toy. Parents who make these types of comments are not intentionally trying to harm their child, it's just the way we have been trained to think. Which is why renewing the mind and changing the way we think about gender roles is so essential. Renewing the mind may sound spiritual, and in my opinion, it is. But renewing the mind also takes daily work. Affirming a little girl's worth and teaching her to self-love, speak up for herself, and not apologize for being and wanting different, are all steps to renewed thinking. Our focus should be on raising healthy girls not raising moms. We don't esteem self and well being as early and as often as we should. Young girls are watching and looking to us for guidance. We can continue to accept antiquated ideas, or we can give them options. The option to change the trajectory of their journey. The option to step out of their circumstance and create their own lane. Having options create balance and I am sure we can all agree that balance is a good thing.

If the first set of questions did not sound familiar, you might be part of, what I like to call, my *unique* sisters. Instead, we may have pondered these questions and concerns. What if I don't want to have babies? Will I be enough? Do I have to have kids to be a "real" woman? Does parenting fulfill everyone? Is pregnancy the only goal for marriage? Will children provide unconditional love? Is it their job to give it to me? Will having a baby make the father love me more? What if I regret having children? Is something wrong with me if I don't want to be a mother? Will other women judge me because of my decision? So many questions that don't get answered or discussed because we would rather preserve a "dream" that suggest there's only one path to reach your destiny.

If you're more likely to ask the second set of questions, then you are not alone! A lot of us have other ideas for our lives that do not consist of becoming a mother or getting married for that matter. Some of us would rather travel the unbeaten path. The majority may consider us atypical because we want to set the tone and posture for our own idea of what it means to be a "real" woman. The American culture has formed and influenced so much of our thinking and beliefs. Renewing our minds to think in a whole new way sounds simple in theory but in reality it takes persistence. Not only the culture, but religion has played a large role in how we view ourselves. In some religions, women are still frowned upon for wearing pants, go figure! Believe it or not, women are still unable to become ministers or leaders of the church, according to certain religions. So having roles is an ingrained part of our history, for sure. There's nothing wrong with having roles, its just that women haven't been part of the decision making process nearly enough. We were put in a box to cook, clean, have and raise babies, submit to the man, be strong for everybody, look your best, and don't complain.

I believe the word for it is…. superwoman!

Well, let's be honest and totally transparent. NO ONE lives that life! Not you, not me, not any celebrity on television (at least not without paid help). So when society determined a "real" woman should be and do all of these things, I jumped off the boat and started swimming in uncharted waters. Yes, it may be easier to stay the course and follow the route that has been paved for us for centuries. After all, it would not require the bravery and fearlessness to stand alone. My decision to be child-free often left me feeling alone in my earlier years. But as I get older and more confident, I look back at my younger self and thank her for owning her decision. I am profoundly grateful to God for always filling me up with what I may have thought I was missing out on. He is faithful. Writing your own narrative does have its difficulties but it also comes with the license and liberty to create a beautiful life with no limitations.

Perpetuating this idea of a "real woman" can be detrimental to our young girls. Consequently, they will continue to believe that having babies will magically fulfill them or even keep their relationship together. Most of these young girls are following their inherited paths, what they see around them or view on social media. Too many do not even view life as optional. What you are born into is not the only option. What your mother or grandmother went through is not your journey. Yes, we must acknowledge the past and absolutely learn from it but in no way does that mean we have to repeat it. We have options and making yourself a priority is one of them. This child-free lifestyle is not taught or shown to us the way motherhood is shown. Instead, this lifestyle is often paired with sadness and longing, depression and desperation. What if we show a different side to being child-free? What if we make movies about child-free women who are totally satisfied and enjoying life? What if we make the main character a child-free woman that isn't waiting for her DAY? Everyday can be her day! It may seem difficult to imagine this but it is so possible. Changing the way we view life and understanding what truly counts is nothing short of a miracle. Give yourself permission to do it differently. You may still decide to follow the beaten path and that is okay. CF life is not for everybody, just know that your thinking can make or break where your journey takes you.

This unbeaten path can lead to the street called Loneliness, the road of Confusion, and down a side street of Disobedience. It may be filled with unknown turns, hills to climb, and detours leading you in the wrong direction for a few miles (or years) but what life doesn't? Don't beat yourself up. What doesn't kill you does make you stronger just don't forget to pull over, breathe (inhale through your nose for 5, exhale through your mouth for 5), regroup, then press the gas. Don't get stuck, You got this!

Once you've braved through the rough trenches and wrong turns (as you will with any path you take), set your eyes on the north star. You are well on your way to Peace Boulevard which leads to the Highway of Happiness and through the Trails of Pleasure. It's all about how you embrace it. And of course, how you think about your life. Are you focusing on what you do not have or being grateful for what you do have? Our thinking is so powerful, which is why it is so hard to change. You can wake up and claim it is going to be a bad day, or you can wake up and give thanks. Either way, your thinking WILL guide your day.

Old thinking suggests that the only way women can be fruitful and multiply is by having children. People might use scripture to make you feel as though being fruitful has one path and that's through your womb. Not! Being fruitful represents so many things. Yes, one way is definitely through your womb. But if we really understand scripture, we know that being fruitful is manifested in areas of our lives that are not connected to our anatomy. Our responsibilities stretch far beyond our wombs. I will discuss more of this topic in Step 6, keep reading. If we are to be a part of a larger body (plan) that impacts generations to come,we must understand that planting seeds is not just for your blood family. Planting seeds and nourishing soil throughout our circles of influence is just as important to being fruitful. As my pastor, Dr. Warren Stewart Sr. says, "sow some seeds and saturate your circle." We all have the responsibility of being fruitful, no matter how small our circle may be. Just like a forest cannot thrive with just one type of plant (seed), neither can we. There needs to be a variety of seeds planted to make the forest resourceful and beautiful, each seed having its own significance. Know that you are doing what you're supposed to be doing. Don't let anyone tell you that you are not being blessed because (fill in the blank). Not true. God chose you! Your seed IS valuable!

Unfortunately, we are constantly comparing our lives to what we think is the perfect life. We spend so much of our time trying to reach a certain status, thinking it will finally make our lives complete. We've been told which life will bring contentment and satisfaction. And I have to disagree. Life is so complex and filled with uncertainty, there's isn't a quick fix. This journey is meant for us to question the norms and flourish.

As far back in history as you and I can remember, we have been given one idea of success. There has been no room for detours or diversion. This seems to be a pattern in our great country. A country that without a doubt could use some adjustments and repairs. I encourage young ladies to steer history into herstory.

2020 has brought about a lot of things, good and bad, but for me it has brought a sense of responsibility. Even more so than I felt prior to. 2020 has made me look at my sisters through different lenses. We are a force ladies and no matter what our paths may be, we have to stick together and encourage one another to live life unapologetically on our own terms. It is very clear, that our voices are powerful and need to be heard. When we speak, the world listens.

We each have the power, responsibility and

permission to travel our own journey and honor our best self.

Now, unfortunately some will say that I am telling women that God doesn't want them to reproduce and multiply. Others may even make me out to be some type of "bitter anti-reproductive baby hater" which are both bogus. If you know me you know that is so far from the truth. I'm okay with folks who don't understand or agree with my position. I'm not writing a book to get "followers" or "likes." I know this is a taboo subject and most people don't want to stir the pot or challenge what we consider normal for women. My truth comes from my story, my life, and my experiences. I know there are women out there who don't want to become mothers or can't become mothers. Perhaps they waited too late and subsequently didn't become mothers or have any other personal reason why becoming a mother was not their journey or priority. This book is for you . . . Not only is this book for my CF sisters but also for the mothers that are raising daughters. It may help you understand her unique perspective, so you can be supportive rather than disappointed that perhaps, your dreams won›t come true. With all due respect, she deserves options. Perhaps you did have babies and now they are out of the house and you are empty nesting with just you and your feelings, this book is for you as well. With love.

I lived with the isolation and frustration that comes with our choice to forego parenthood. I understand the challenges you'll have to go through or have gone through by opting out. I know the judgement people pass because you haven't been called "Mom." It's almost as if we have to continually remind people that we are still valuable humans with so much to offer. But I also know the contentment and joy that comes from honoring your truth. I know the satisfaction that is gained when you are loved for simply being you, and not what you can give. I have learned that people, family or not, cannot bring the kind of fulfillment that only God can give. I do not want to sound cliché, but it is so true. It's an intimate type of joy that is worth nurturing. However you choose to nurture that relationship is up to you, but I would defintely reccommend starting (or continuing). Renewing your mind begins with intention. Believing in yourself and reminding yourself that you can control what you think about. Speaking kinder words to yourself and not seeking validation from external sources. Daily practice and prayer can all change your mindset. This journey is between you and God! Period!

From shattering glass ceilings, to voting rights, to the Me Too movement, women have been responsible for changing societal ideology since day one. They have been innovators, and continue to be at the forefront galvanizing progressive movements in this country and all over the world. Whether they were mothers or not, their ability to surpass institutionalized thinking proves our significance is much more than motherhood alone. I love us, all women; young, mature, single, married, CF, mothers, and everything in between. I love our hearts, our laughter, our boldness and our many shapes and sizes covered in the most rich and radiant hues. I am the product of a fierce, educated, beautiful woman, inside and out. If it weren't for my mother and God's grace, I wouldn't be the woman I am today. I am so grateful that she gave me a real-life example of what a loving, phenonmeal, spiritually guided woman looks like. The foundation she laid for me, positively made a difference. Without a doubt, those are qualities that have propelled me to thrive and move forward in my own life.

And speaking of my queen, I would be remiss if I didn't share a story of how she shaped my relationship with Jesus at an early age. I believe she actually helped renew my mind before it became a thing. Being that I grew up in the church, I learned about God very early on. My mom made sure we attended church every Sunday, so it was just a part of my life. But on this particular day, I remember it like it was yesterday. I was about 9-10 years old and I was known for sleeping with my mom almost every night when she'd allow it, lol. I would try anything (sickness, fear, sadness) just to crawl into her luxurious bed and fall asleep before she could kick me out! One night I couldn't fall asleep in my own bed, so I walked out to the living room, where my mom was watching television. I told her I couldn't sleep because I was scared and asked if I could just go lay in her room for awhile. Well, to my surprise, she replied, "No....how about you go back to your own bed and say Jesus over and over until you fall asleep." Shocked and hurt, I rolled my eyes (discretely, of course) and walked myself back down the hallway to my room and climbed into my white, cold, lonely canopy bed. I laid there and whispered Jesus, Jesus, Jesus until I fell asleep. I don't recall how many times I said it or how long it took me but I do know that I continued calling His name. The next morning, I remember waking up in my own bed feeling some kind of way. Instead of feeling let down by my mom, a sense of confidence and comfort filled me that I hadn't felt before. From that day forward, I believe, my spiritual relationship was developing. It taught me that God is even bigger than my mom and when I don't know what else to do, call on Jesus! That was the beginning of my very personal relationship with God. I haven't stopped talking to Him since. I get so much comfort in knowing He is always with me, I feel it! And for that, I am so grateful for my beautiful mother.

With that being said, it doesn't negate that fact that not all women have to be mothers or even want to be mothers. Many girls grow up wanting to be a better mother than their own mom was to them. They think if they can just have a baby, they will not only prove a point but fill a void as well. Our upbringing usually plays a direct role in our behavior as an adult. To think you will undo/fix your childhood by having your own kids is a distortion of thinking (optical illusion) that too many women believe and find out the the hard way. When I hear mothers say, "I can't wait for you to have kids so they can put you through it, like you do to me" is kind of sad. It's another subconscious message to your daughter. I'm sure most parents say it jokingly but it still sends a message. First, it is assuming they are going to become a parent. Secondly, implying motherhood is a payback rather than an opportunity to pay it forward. Becoming a mother should be a choice and one that is made with clear lenses. Being child-free should also be a clear choice. If you feel like the world owes you something or you missed your opportunity as a child to be happy, I would strongly suggest holding off on parenthood and taking time to learn you! Who are you? What is your purpose? What gifts can you offer? What is your motive? How can you become the best you without needing a child to fill a void? You may very well still decide to become a parent and that is beautiful, but you may also decide to opt out and trust me, that is beautiful as well. You may realize so much about yourself that you will have to share it with others and bless others with your story. Self discovery is a gift in itself.   Whether you are a mother or a child-free woman, self-discovery is so necessary. We have so much more to celebrate than motherhood alone. We are the soul of this nation. Us women must unite and support one another and be inclusive of each other's lives and choices. We can all be real women, not based on what we have but because of who we are! For far too long, society has used "motherhood" to divide us. Quite frankly, it's not just the haves and the have nots. It's even mothers versus mothers in some cases. Breastfeeding versus formula and which mom is viewed more worthy. A child-free woman who is young versus a CF woman who is older. There are many ways women are divided and my desire is to be part of the solution, not the problem. Why don't men have to deal with so much division? Why is it okay for a man to not have kids and still live a productive, fulfilling life? Why don't men get pressured like women do? Why aren't there any deadlines and age cutoffs for men? How come they aren't expected to live up to certain standards in order to be considered "real" men? Why? Because this doesn't exist for them. For the most part, men can do what they want, with whom they want, when they want, and not be questioned. I'm fine with that—just let us women live our lives as well. There's no competition, just a need for cohesiveness and appreciation.

Being that our world is hyper masculine, women who think like me have not been valued or highly regarded. Changing the way you think about your role or responsibility in life can be very scary. Especially when it comes to your identity and how the world views you. Females who opt out of the mother role are often discounted and viewed as less than. Unfortunately not enough guidance and attention is given to the young lady who decides to take ownership of her "not so popular" position. Ladies who live their lives unapologetically. My sisters that are caregivers to many but mothers to none. Brave women who shower other people's kids with love and quality time. Those that listen attentively, give without expectations, donate services, pray for, lift up and perform countless other deeds that go unnoticed and unspoken of by society. These are exceptional women who far too often get ignored and overlooked. My intent is to shine a light on these treasured women. Women with beautiful souls who are quick to be labeled "selfish" by so many. They are truly blessings and should be in high demand, especially in these crazy times we are living in. These women are prized aunties, priceless godmothers, dedicated mentors, intelligent daughters, sisters and friends. They are creative geniuses and trailblazers. Women who most definitely deserve to be recognized as the real women they are! These women are me and because I am her,

I owe it to my brave sisters to share my journey from self-condemnation to satisfaction and beyond! I owe it to the unconventional girl that needs a different road map to follow.

This ride will take you off the beaten pathway but when you reach your destination, you will understand the exclusive excursion you were given to enjoy. Sit back!

Renewing your mind doesn't happen overnight. As with any investment it takes time, consistency, determination, and strong faith. Consistency is doing something every day. It doesn't have to be something big, but it has to be something uplifting to your soul daily. We are more likely to stick to something when we make it a routine. Renewing your mind is no different. You have to be willing to challenge the thinking that may feel more comfortable, in order to open your mind to new possibilities. It's the mindset, the feelings, the lies that control us if we're not careful. If we want to renew our thinking, we have to take control of our mind first. The mindset will follow. Make a promise to invest in yourself one day at a time. It will add up, trust!

We must be determined to live a life we're proud of, a life we are appreciative of, and a life with a legacy. Be patient with yourself and be forgiving. Mistakes will happen and that's to be expected, they are always an opportunity to learn and grow. Use those mistakes to add meaning and purpose to your life, which will aid in defining who you are. With this knowledge you are more equipped to set goals and design the path you desire. According to research, nearly 80 percent of people never reach the goals they set for themselves. Setting goals is one thing, but actually concentrating your efforts to get there is what brings the goal to fruition. Goal setting is not limited to school and career, setting life goals keeps you focused and less likely to be distracted.

In life and definitely in this country (even when it is evident that something isn't working) we have a tendency to continue with the familiar and falsely claim it is working; a law, a policy, an institution. Leaders have not been transparent in taking accountability or exposing secrets that account for a lot of dysfunction in our world, from the white house to our family homes. In some cases, it's just easier not to talk about certain topics because it may contradict the message that we've inherited. Changing our mindset will definitely open up a whole new world of possibilities and opportunities. The opportunity to right some wrongs.

For example, using my educational background, the mindset that children will turn 5 and automatically be kindergarten ready is false. Yet, year after year, we continue to witness the learning gap increase because of failed efforts to make education equitable for all. There are some parents who don't understand the importance of being your child's first teacher and preparing them for success way before they start kindergarten. A tremendous amount of work has to be put in when you make such a critical commitment. A lot of parents know that raising a child begins at birth (before actually), but with so many kids at a disadvantage entering school, it has to be talked about. The learning gap is real and a major factor in closing it, is parents understanding how crucial their role is. Unfortunately, young kids are learning about adult issues at home rather than developing age-appropriate language and literacy skills. Prior to starting kindergarten, a few skills a child should have are being able to say and spell their name, identify numbers and understand that letters represent sounds. Children should be able to self-regulate and express themselves appropriately. They should be read to daily to build their vocabulary. These are skills that will set a child up for academic success. Education begins at home, not school. What your child learns or does not learn at home will almost always make its way into the classroom. I've heard eight-year-olds comment about how depressed or stressed out they are. In actuality, they are just mirroring what they see and hear at home. As a teacher, I have witnessed my share of dysfunction that is wrong on so many levels. It starts with adults but if we aren't willing to change our mindset, renew our thinking and set new expectations, we will continue to get the same results; a broken world.

Perhaps, if we change the narrative, new voices can

be heard. Dare to try a different path. If we continue to get the same results, for example, in education, then a new perspective is warranted and can be pivotal. In our country, we have another mindset that perpetuates a cycle known as the school to prison pipeline. The criminal justice system is counting on the educational system to fail to determine how much funding needs to be allocated to incarcerate black and brown males. I mean, what in the dysfunctional world is going on? Institutional racism is absolutely real, yet we've been accustomed to being silent. We must talk about change and renewing the way we think about so many things. We have to start viewing life totally different. A child-free lifestyle for many is contributing to the greater good and shouldn't be viewed any different than that.

With so much dysfunction in the world, having strong faith is also a must in renewing one's mind. Believing that you can do it all on your own, will surely lead to negative thinking. Now it may begin as tiny faith (mustard seed faith), but trust me, even that's enough! As you grow and stay consistent, your faith also grows stronger and your thinking gets renewed over and over. Yes, you'll have days or seasons when you "feel" like all your faith is gone. Well, don't always listen to your feelings; they are not always speaking truth. A lot of times our feelings are what get us into trouble. Stay focused and ask God to increase your faith. Speak life to yourself, even in those difficult times. It works! Be consistent, intentional, and faithful. And, make sure you slow down and breathe. Something so natural as breathing can be a game changer when it's done with intentionality.

We have the power to think about how awful we are and point out all of our flaws causing us to feel depressed and unworthy. Or, we can use our power to speak life, with positive affirmations, gratitude and showing ourself a little grace every single day.

Focus on the positive but pay attention to the negative thoughts. Be intentional when talking to your negative thoughts. Most of what we see and hear on a daily basis does not feed our souls. It is our responsibility to encourage ourselves. One. negative. thought. at. a. time. When a thought comes in our mind that does not align with positivity, change it! Stop! Acknowledge it! And say something kinder and more conscious to yourself. I would actually suggest saying the word, NO out loud, to verbally stop the thought(s), and speak something positive (out loud) about yourself. Even if you don't believe it or it sounds corny, replace that thought. Your faith relies on your thinking and your thinking relies on your faith. Like my friend use to say, "change your mind, change your life." I couldn't agree more.

There are so many people who think what they own or have or even children will complete them and give them the satisfaction they are so desperately looking for. This is so far from the truth. Children are blessings and can add to the fulfillment you already have. They are not created to give it to you. It took some time to realize my fulfillment was inside of me even when I had nothing and no one else to fill me. Because of a strong foundation, I always turned my attention upward to feel complete. We can only truly gain peace, joy, contentment, and self-love when we do the daily work. Then we can live our best lives and in turn live in a healthier, more compassionate world. We can raise healthier children with vigorous minds, which leads to more confident, competent, and caring adults.

Renewing your mind may come off as righteous or maybe impractical to you, I get it. We aren't taught how to take ownership of our minds and think on purpose as much as we are shown and told what to think. We'd rather let someone else do the thinking for us. I want to express to young ladies everywhere that you have the power to change your story. You have the power to change your thinking. You most certainly have the power to change your life by renewing your mind.

Step 2

EXAMINING YOUR FEELINGS

SONG
"TIME WILL REVEAL"
DEBARGE

NOW THAT WE'VE discussed renewing your mind and changing the way you see yourself, BE PREPARED to have disrespectful feelings arise, and question or second guess your new mindset more often than not. Examining and acknowledging these feelings will be part of the journey. There's no way around it. Learning to feel and respond accordingly is a lifelong process for many people but it does get easier.

What I've discovered over the years with journaling and the practice of being present is that the strategies don't change much. It is usually my willingness to apply them that changes from time to time. That's why I have learned to be consistent with my breathing practices and my quiet time; my intimate time with God. Believe it or not, my mind is not always in educator mode, I am very much an intricate woman, like most of us. It's one thing to know, it's a whole new world to apply. Although I'm a teacher, I generally do not come from a "scholarly" or studious place, using a lot of fancy words and stats. I write from my heart and if I have to say it ten different times to make my point, I do. Sometimes repetition is the best way to make information stick. So forgive me in advance if I recycle information and techniques throughout my book. I tend to keep things straightforward and simple. When it works it just works!

Examining your feelings as a child-free woman will help you differentiate external and internal emotions. For example, being angry at "them" versus owning and forgiving. Your journey has not been taken by many, and quite frankly, not talked about by many, so don't expect others to understand or empathize with you. Most people can't even fathom why you've chosen to live CF. You see, for most, not having children wasn't even a thought because no one talks about this viable option with pride and joy. Society does not celebrate or honor this lifestyle, therefore denying permission to be different. Having a baby is something that majority of girls view as their obligation. Other girls grew up with the understanding that all girls have babies so it is inevitable that it would happen to them one day. When the decision to become sexually active arose, most of us embodied our concupiscent nature and didn't think twice about becoming a mother. Most of us had NO business even becoming sexually active, let alone a mother to a whole human being. We were all about our feelings and blinded by ignorance. And without stepping too far out of my lane, sex does not have to equal baby. Let's be transparent with our youth because we know simply telling our girls to keep their legs shut is not necessarily going to go over well. Remember when you were told that? Honest communication seems to lend the best results. Talk about the value of their bodies. Have conversations about ownership and what it means to protect their body, heart, soul, and freedom for that matter.

The emotional roller coaster ride from our teens to well beyond our twenties greatly impacts our decision making ability. At this stage in life, our feelings seem to take over all rational reasoning. Our choices during this fragile season can sustain or impact the rest of our lives. Why not offer new and improved tools that may possibly change the trajectory of our younger girl's paths? Focus on our feelings and understand how much control we actually have. Address how emotions can and do destroy lives. Good choices lead us down certain paths and bad choices lead us down others. This is when it is pivotal to develop lifelong strategies that will help navigate your journey. Choose wisely. Be selective. Be unapologetic. Be different. Those decades are filled with love, lust, dumb decisions, sex and more feelings than we can handle. Yes, we all lose common sense and become emotional wrecks! During these critical learning years, babies are born left and right to "emotional wreck" girls/women. It is disheartening that young girls are the ones who suffer the most, and most likely left to raise babies alone. Yes, women have done it for years, but does that make it right ? Is it too late to change how we view children in our world? Can we take some of the pressure off of our young women while going through such an emotional stage in life? Can we do better? These are questions I often wonder, especially in my role as a teacher. I have seen how trauma can leave its mark on generations. Neglect, abuse, poverty, anxiety/depression, are all traumas that leave young girls vulnerable. I feel as though I am doing a disservice to girls everywhere if I can't speak candidly about what it means to bring a child in this world. Let's be clear, I am not pointing the finger or blaming moms. I do believe however, regulating our feelings is something that must be taught and modeled. Preparing girls for the overwhelming emotional turmoil that comes alongside womanhood is our obligation. No one else will have the hard conversations and offer alternatives that can promote healthier lifestyles. Remember, we are accustomed to the familiar, the secrets, the traditional ways. Change is a process.

We cannot continue to glorify bringing children into this world and not properly educate our youth about the repercussions of our choices. The job to parent is not for everyone and that is not a judgement, it's called reality. And by the way, doesn't make you any less worthy. There's strength in knowing. I thought it was time for a different perspective, to humbly show the possibilities of being fruitful and blessed while opting out. Not a woman who claims to be better than or have anything close to a perfect life, just a woman with fortitude and grit living my most blessed life.

How about we challenge our young ladies to work on their spiritual, emotional, mental, and physical health during those critical, inquisitive years so they have much more to offer when it's time to make life-long decisions. Let us be the generation that sets new standards and expectations, meant to build our girls up rather than tear them down.

Feelings are so difficult to process. It appears situations and circumstances always catch you off guard. You may be doing just fine, minding your own business one day, then next thing you know, you are at an intersection feeling lost and alone. Your feelings have gotten the best of you and all your hard work seems to have been for nothing. You find yourself angry and questioning all of your decisions. At times, the path gets dark and you can't seem to see what's in front of you. That's typically when our flesh aches for familiarity and comfort. When our deep-seated issues and human nature speak the loudest. What I've learned is that our spiritual being is much quieter, which is why being intentional about listening to it is more challenging for all of us. Our flesh has no problem stepping in and controlling us when we feel lost or frustrated. Not to worry, it happens. Just be aware that the impulsive pull to react is normal but you can harnass it. Again, remember to breathe, inhale for a six count this time and audibly exhale for six, regroup, and tune in. Use this stop as a turning point to examine your feelings and practice being present. What do you smell or hear to bring you back to right now? Tell yourself you are okay. You don't have to feel something in order to do it or say it. Just like you can feel something and not react on it. Pause and acknowlegde the feeling so you can give it a name and deal with it.

As humans, we tend to react as soon as we feel. If it's anger, a lot of us react with yelling or hitting. If it's sadness, some react with crying or isolation. If we feel hurt, we can tend to react by hurting others, but does that truly solve anything? Does it make your feelings disappear? No. We know the feelings are real that you will encounter. We can feel them, but are they true? You may feel like you don't matter but the truth is, you absolutely do. Yes, we need to understand all the different feelings, but we don't need to give them all life. Any journey you embark on will have you feeling like you are alone and unfit, but trust me, if you're breathing, you can not only finish, you can finish strong!

When you lose a loved one isn't it quite normal to go through stages? Denial, bargaining, guilt, anger, depression, and acceptance . . . depending on who you talk to, there may even be a few more stages to grief. These stages are real and the feelings that surface are absolutely real. But our brain and bodies are so complex. What we've experienced in life controls how our brain perceives things. So we can change our feelings with new experiences. Our bodies are resilient, but we are not made to take on all these feelings, stress, anxieties, and heartbreaks and not have an outlet or release. These feelings, if neglected or suppressed, can lead to physical illness, infections, diseases, and even death. I'm using grief because I know most of us have experienced this and can relate to the emotions that come alongside those feelings.

When feelings are left unattended, whether, from grieving or a choice we make, they can inflict major damage. Denial, bargaining, guilt, anger, depression, jealousy, overthinking, doubt, and yes, acceptance, are all part of this decision and lifestyle, but just like grief you can conquer those feelings and turn them into fuel for your journey. We all experience trauma and situations that were meant to break us. Unfortunately, it's part of life, but there is good news. It's really not about the circumstance we're in. It's more about how we think of that circumstance and whether we choose to be proactive or reactive. It is a choice.

Are you willing to be proactive about your life, taking time to learn you, setting goals, making decisions that benefit your future? Or reactive, just *waiting* for things to happen? Waiting for someone to do this, so you can do that. Giving someone else authority over your happiness. Trust me, being proactive takes more effort but the payoff is so rewarding. I'm not saying every day will be filled with joy and you'll be walking around smiling from ear to ear. You'll have bad moments, days, and seasons, but if I'm going to be honest, my good days outweigh my bad days by a long shot. As a matter of fact, I don't remember the last time my entire day was ruined. Well, actually, I can: witnessing George Floyd's murder on television. That shook me for some time, but even then, before I laid down to sleep, I gave thanks to my Lord and Savior Jesus Christ. Not for what the cold-hearted, evil cop did to him, but because his death would not be in vain and would begin the healing of a broken nation.

That is not to say I don't feel sad, angry, betrayed, and a multitude of other feelings on any given day. I am human, it's normal. I just know that I can change my feelings with my thoughts when my feelings are not serving me.

Like I mentioned before, it's not that our bodies can't handle feelings; we just want to make sure feelings are not handling us! Some stress is considered good, but our bodies can't take continual stress. We can handle some anxiety, as a matter of fact, some anxiety is good but we were not created to take on persistent anxiety. We can even handle temporary depression, but constant mood swings are unhealthy. Any emotion we experience should be regulated and balanced. Too much of anything can lead to negative outcomes. So when these feelings or stages show themselves in your child-free lifestyle, recognize them, acknowledge them, and then get them under control.

You have the power to steer yourself back onto the right path. As you grow, like all things, it becomes less challenging. You will have hills or mountains to climb, streams to swim up, roadblocks, dead ends, and several U-turns, but with time and growth your path will become clear and before you know it your feelings will no longer have control over you. To paraphrase Pastor Dollar, a man who cannot control his emotions is a weak man. That really stuck and made so much sense to me.

I hope you are feeling more confident about your journey. It's definitely not over but you have more power, right? You can take the scenic route. You can pull over when you want and just breathe, just be. You can play music that speaks to your soul. You can roll the windows down or blast the heat, whatever floats your boat. This is your journey, your rules. We have one captain, one pilot, and He is all we truly need. Now go and be great queen, do you. The best is yet to come!

With love.

Step 3
RELEASING JUDGEMENT

SONG
"DON'T JUDGE ME"
KHIERRA SHEARD FEATURING MISSY ELLIOT

HERE ARE A few more questions you might have to face:

What will people think of me? Will they think I'm selfish? Will they assume something is wrong with me? Will I be judged as a woman? Will relationships change? Will I not be asked to hang out anymore? Are there other women that share my stance on this?

Let me answer a few of those for you. People will think you're weird and secretly assume you are selfish. They will definitely judge and quite possibly exclude you from social gatherings. Oh, and yes they will think something might be wrong with you. They might even feel like it is their duty to fix you. Perhaps, they will attempt to pry into your business and ask questions like, "Do you plan on having kids in the future?", "Would you consider a surrogate?", "Have you tried (fill in the blank)?" In my earlier years it was a lot more difficult for me to find the words to keep it cool. Most questions are just followed with expecting eyes and a fake smile, like they're waiting for you to convert. In my experience, a lot of people just aren't ready for a firm, "we just don't want children" answer. Sometimes there's an uncomfortable silence, but it's all good. We need to feel uncomfortable every now and then. It can cause folks to reflect and possibly ask different questions.

I'm pretty sure that most of us who chose to forego motherhood are the minority in our circle. Whether your circle is family, coworkers, neighbors, or friends, most likely, you are outnumbered. We are typically "the one" who doesn't have children. If your circle is larger, you may be in the great company of two or three like sisters. Woohoo, that's awesome and more support than most of us have or had. But it's all good, I'm here to bring us together so we can support and empower our extraordinary sisters.

When we don't have support, no matter what the support is for, our feelings and thoughts become that much more difficult to master. When folks start to pressure you or pass judgement, you feel isolated and vulnerable. Support is just a natural part of humanity. Think about addicts, for example, when they attend AA/NA, it's not to get a magic pill and be healed, it's for support. When you're on a diet, programs like NOOM and Weight Watchers offer support. If you are part of a fitness group, the people in the group motivate, encourage, and support one another. Mothers and expecting mothers have multiple support groups, books, clubs, blogs—you name it. You can search for any one of these groups and find hundreds of support systems set up and created for the sole purpose of offering support. Being successful at something is a lot more doable when you have a village, a tribe, a system set up for reinforcement. We are stronger together.

But wait . . . what about us? What about support groups that understand the challenges we face? This lifestyle, although it comes with lots of freedom and independence, can also lead to destruction, or losing one's soul trying to find meaning. This lifestyle is filled with benefits, but like anything, there's a downside. Similar to any lifestyle, if it doesn't affect you, you don't really get it. And when people don't get it or understand it, they are quick to judge. We may not deal with the daily demands of parenthood, but that doesn't mean we don't experience our own struggles. Living CF isn't for everyone. You will have to develop thick skin to handle some of the harsh and inconsiderate comments and norms that have been acceptable over the years. Finding your place to fit in may be challenging but with new normal being created everyday, I'm hopeful that CF life will earn its respect in our world. That's why I emphasize that with this lifestyle it is essential to have structure, daily routine, and support. Who better can identify with you than another CF woman? We need like-minded friends and mentors to guide and offer counsel along the way. It's important to have ladies that you can laugh with, break bread with, pray with, and get away with. Skeptics are out there and will definitely *try it*. Having a squad makes a difference. Until you find that circle, I hope this book will give you hope. One day we can come together (Zoom or in person) and celebrate US! That is definitely a goal of mine.

I know how offensive the world can be. How offputting some people are without even recognizing it. How our society downplays a woman's autonomy. The history of turning something positive into a negative if it's not beneficial to them. I know how curious people are and that everyone does not respect our privacy when it comes to not wanting children. It's almost like people automatically go into detective mode. It may seem like common sense to most of us not to pry, but trust me, some people have no filter and dive right in. Let's keep it basic when meeting someone new and not go straight to personal digging when you find out she doesn't have kids. I'm almost certain that you wouldn't even have to ask. Being child-free is not an open invitation to find out "what's wrong." Not wanting a baby doesn't mean something is wrong, perhaps, something is right. Fortunately, it is becoming more popular and acceptable. I know ladies today are taking their time and not feeling as much pressure to have babies, the way I did. Get to know a woman on an introductory level before trying to figure out why she doesn't have kids. If and when she feels comfortable, she can divulge as much or as little personal information as she wishes.

At work, the salon, waiting for an appointment, there should be boundaries. I shouldn't know your medical history after talking to you for ten minutes. I enjoy getting to know all types of people. I enjoy building realtionships and genuinely care about the well-being of others. But there is a difference between getting to know someone casually and digging to be nosy. It's not necessary to forge conversations just for the sake of talking. Some of us introverts would rather not.

I digress, back to judgement. The comments and questions come from a place of curiosity and ignorance. Clearly the inclusion of CF women has not been part of the conversation. And if it was, most likely, it was told by someone that didn't have children but longing to do so. Which in that case, I think the term childless is more appropriate. I do not want to speak for all women who don't have kids. Certainly, there are women who desire nothing more than to have a baby and can not! I want to be clear, I have empathy for my childless sisters for sure. I don't want to gloss over the fact that there is no one way, one story, one answer. I do know that I am not alone and women like me no longer have to be silenced.

Being judgmental is a part of human nature. We all do it. So yes, you will be judged for your decision to opt out of being a mother. This is extremely difficult for some to wrap their heads around but that's why it's necessary for us to use our voices. Don't let their issues become your issues. Don't let the pressure and stress weigh you down. People can be relentless and we have to remember most of them don't know any better.

After I got married, people wasted no time asking when the babies were coming. With all seriousness, folks started inquiring literally days after the wedding. How many kids do you want? When are you going to start working on baby #1? Time to start pushing out babies! I mean, it was immediate and I have to say, very intrusive. When I would tell people we didn't want kids, the look I received was a combination of bewilderment and shock. Almost as if the option to marry for love and companionship was unacceptable and confusing. I am aware that most people who marry start a family. I just don't think it's okay to assume or judge when it's done differently. It goes back to the standards and expectations that have been ingrained. A perfect example of this came from a family friend (older male) when I was around 33 years old attending a birthday party for one of my cousins. He wanted to know why my husband and I didn't have kids. When I told him that we didn't plan on having any, he replied, "how old are you?" I reluctantly told him my age and his response was, "oh that's why you don't have kids, you waited too long and now you're too old." And with no shame, he went on about his business as if it was his right to have an opinion about my uterus. I was not only bothered by his comment but upset with myself that I didn't have a good clapback to shut him up. I did inform him that thirty-three was not too old to have a baby IF that's what I wanted. Unfortunately, these type of comments leave scars and can negatively alter a person's self image. That's when having control over your emotions really comes in handy. Not every comment deserves a lashing nor does every action require a reaction.

The autonomy of women having control over their bodies always gets lost in the chaos of our male-dominated world. Why is it that men enforce what we will or will not do? Until we impart new boundaries for our bodies, we will continue to be subjected to their antiquated thinking and confirming preventive cycles.

What cycles, you ask? Praising and celebrating pregnancy without advocating and expecting greatness after birth. As a society we are quick to create television shows around teen pregnancy or post pictures of celebrities showing adorable baby bumps. We highlight the "bounce back" as if having babies is a seamless, easy process.We send out the illusion that it's all about the pregnancy and not the parenting. Young girls are watching. Pregnancy is beautiful indeed, so let's not minimize it to only what the body can do without maximizing what the mom has to do afterward.

It's not enough to have private conversations about babies having babies or gossiping about it. It's not right to look down on children who aren't being raised adequately and just throw out insulting comments. We can't continue to overlook the fact that far too many girls are repeating these damaging cycles and not offer alternatives or solutions. We have to be open and honest about parenting. I know I may get a lot of backlash from this but my intention, truly, is to help our girls not hurt them. Yes, I do believe that children are blessings. I also believe that not having children can be a blessing as well. When others use the term selfish, I see it as selfless. When I think about the hard conversations that parents must have with their black sons (and daughters), the horrible drug epidemic that is ruining so many young lives, and social media which has engulfed kids' lives, I see child-free as a sacrifice for many. These concerns are all of ours. In some way, shape, or form every child will experience trauma but why not give our future leaders a different opportunity to experience the world without so much struggle?

Options. Yet we continue to say kids are resilient . . . they'll be all right. Yes, I agree, children are resilient but again, does that make it right? Child protective services are overwhelmed and many are not properly trained to handle the cases that are reported. Women who have been abused and are broken themselves are having babies and not getting the help or support they need to become whole. These are cycles that go unnoticed and babies are being born into it daily. We are all aware that children grow into adults and if we can't talk honestly, unhealthy cycles continue to shape our society. If we speak about the responsibilities of parenthood honestly, future generations can make better informed decisions about the path they choose to travel. In my profession, I engage with hundreds of students every year, and saying that we have to do better is an understatement. Children who suffer because of selfish parents or parents who don't know any better are most likely going to repeat behaviors and traumas that will have punitive consequences later. The list of "whys" concerning the importance of offering options and new perspectives should be largely sought after. I could go on and on with what I've witnessed over the years and it truly breaks my heart! We have to do better!

There's another great quote that sticks with me that we don't refer to, in my opinion, as often as we should. Maybe it should even be the foundation by which we live and establish our families. Fredrick Douglas stated,

"It is easier to build strong children than to repair broken men."

I'll let that sink in....It is absolutely powerful!

So if we choose to be child free and not become a part of an unjust system, then let them judge all they want. But let's be very clear, the issues will not magically disappear because we don't talk about them. I am at a place where I can either stay silent about what is going on or be willing to go against the grain and open up delicate yet unavoidable dialogue that is long overdue.

We need to have high expectations for the hardest job on the planet. Most jobs and careers have higher expectations than we have for parenthood. What's wrong with this picture? Getting pregnant is just the beginning. The ability and responsibility that comes with being an effective parent must be the focus. Let's reverse unfit parenting to capable parenting that every child deserves.

In the education field, there are teacher expectations that are tied to salary. We expect teachers to educate, mediate, counsel, diagnose, intervene, comfort, advise and build meaningful relationships with 20-30 students at the same time. Not to mention, the expectation to have all students passing reading, math, writing and science statewide assessments. The expectations don't change when a teacher has a student that may be performing two grades below his/her grade level. The expectations remain the same, show proficiency and growth for all of your students in order to qualify for incentive pay. In the financial sector, the expectations are to recruit and retain clients, as well as manage the movement of funds. In health and medicine, there are expectations to properly diagnose, inform, treat, and mend a number of health conditions and ailments. All jobs have high expectations, and parenting should be no different. I know there are no "rules" when it comes to parenting but we can be better prepared and set the standards high. I am an advocate for mental health and lifestyle (parenting, CF life, financial literacy, sex ed., etc) courses being offered in high school, if not middle school. Being successful in life should be just as important if not more, than being successful in business. Adulting is not easy and it has more complexity than we once understood. I am no expert in parenting, obviously, but I am an educator with a responsibility to the future generations. If not now, when?

In many homes, respect, appropriate communication, proper discipline, compassion, structure, and good old-fashioned manners, are not taught or modeled anymore. Why? A lot has to do with what we were shown in our own homes and some has to do with common sense or the lack of. We can continue down the same road or we can focus on raising healthier human beings and heal our nation one child at a time. Let us make that judgement call, to break cycles and do our part to benefit the children who are here and those following behind. They don't get to pick their parents. Let's advocate for them. We can break cycles and trauma.

So Judgement doesn't have to be a bad thing. People will judge us for one thing or another and we just have to know in our hearts that our decision isn't harming anyone. Your decision is yours to make, just like parents decide TO have children. And as difficult as it may be, try not to allow judgements to alter your thinking. There's always things we can't control, so what we can, we should. We also can't control other people's opinions. Just stay in your lane and don't be distracted.

We make judgements daily. Remember, even Jesus was judged, and God is still up for debate for many. Whether they come to the conclusion that it's all a big conspiracy theory or they make judgements about us believers being weak, so many people are skeptical. They have their reasons for not believing and quite frankly, some are valid. Many religions have left a vile taste in people's mouth. They've developed resentment and are not open to the idea that religion and spirituality are two different things. Our country has not done a good job representing Godly love. I grew up in the church but I am not religious. When many people think of church, they imagine polished, angelic people with boring lives. People who think they are better than or without flaws. Well, these stereotypes are about religion, not spirituality. I will be the first to admit that I do not have it all together and neither do the people who go to church every Sunday. That is a myth and so far from the truth. My faith and intimate relationship with Jesus Christ doesn't make me perfect, it makes Him perfect for me. I've learned to put my trust in Him and from my experience He has never failed. When I try to figure it all out on my own, I end up doubting myself which leaves me feeling lost and unsure. I find myself trying to please people as oppose to pleasing God. I find myself anxious and worried, rather than trusting and resting. See, people will always debate whether or not God is real. My answer, He is real to me! If I have the choice to live life according to the world or according to the Word, I choose the latter. To me it's a no brainer. The word encourages me to have a life I can be proud of. It inspires me to love and be a light for others. The world is a dark place that will suck the life right out of you. A meaningful life with purpose just feels right. When I die and find out the truth, I can guarantee, I'll have zero regrets about living my best spiritual life. It's a win win! Depending on God is not a sign of weakness, it's a sign of humility and courage. Respecting the fact that you are not as strong as you may want to be and that's okay. If you are willing to take a chance and trust God genuinely, he will reveal the absolute best part of you.

Life will always bring challenges and being judged for one thing or another is part of it. Especially these days when social media is so prevalent. It creates an environment for others to define or judge us without even knowing us. Focus on what is important and what you can control. You can control what you permit in and on your devices. If it doesn't uplift you, don't waste your energy. Most people passing judgment don't even know you. God knows everything about you and still loves you. You don't have to have it all together for Him. Eventually your actions will also align with His if you are intentional and patient with yourself.

We like to use the term, "it is what it is," as if we can't change our outcome (and I understand sometimes we can't) but it doesn't have to be that way when it comes to the life you want to live and your personal choices. You can change the trajectory of your life, one intentional decision at a time. When others pass judgement and they will, focus on Jesus and take back your power. Turbulence may be all around you and you will have an inner peace that is inexplicable and steadfast.

Have you ever met someone who is always pleasant? Always has a light around them, even when they're not trying? Do you know anyone that seems to stay positive even when others around them focus on negativity ALL THE TIME? I can almost guarantee that the person has such strong faith and knows "whose" they are. They can trust and believe that even when they don't have the answers, God is working on their behalf. They know that joy is not external. They probably know that having faith can overpower any negativity and judgement. So their happiness isn't fake, it's intentional.

Even at my age, I must be intentional about passing judgement. The more I focus on my own thoughts, the less time I have to be judgmental of others. Being judged does not always feel good but like I mentioned before, feelings can be dealt with. Acknowledge them and respond accordingly. How you are able to respond shows your strength and resilience. Keep living and you'll realize that judgements and opinions are microscopic in the grander scheme of life. Time is a gift, don't waste it worrying about what others think of you. Look at it like this, if they're judging that means your probably doing something right. Enjoy your life!

"The thief's purpose is to steal and kill and to destroy; My purpose is to give them a rich and satisfying life."
-John 10:10

Step 4

EMBRACING YOUR FREEDOM

SONG
"LIVING MY LIFE LIKE IT'S GOLDEN"
JILL SCOTT

HERE ARE A few more questions and comments you may encounter on this journey:

What do you do with your time? Don't you get bored? Do you ever wonder what kind of mom you would've been? I'd probably drink from morning to night if I didn't have kids! I don't believe my husband and I could stay together if it weren't for our children. You're probably rich, being that you're a DINK (dual income no kids), right? You don't get tired of your husband? Do you ever wonder who will take care of you when you're old?

To a lot of folks, embracing freedom sounds like a no brainer. But when given all the personal freedom you want, it also comes with a price. That's why being intentional is so important. I thrive with structure and routine. Yes, having all this freedom is amazing on most days, but let me break it down.

What do I do with all my time, you ask?

I've learned to cherish every minute of it. Being able to set my own schedule is a blessing that I'm embracing more and more each day. I can get seven to eight hours of peaceful sleep every night and nine hours if it's the weekend or I'm on vacation. People underestimate the power of sleep. Some people even suggest not sleeping, "you can sleep when you're dead" comment that we've all heard or maybe even said. What does that even mean? Is it a badge of honor to not need sleep? Is the ability to function off of 4 hours of sleep supposed to be impressive? I have grown accustomed to peaceful sleep and I wouldn't have it any other way. Sleep is a gift! Research has proven that adequate and proper sleep adds not only years to your life but a healthier, more fit life. The proper amount of sleep relieves stress and anxiety. It also regulates your body's metabolism and provides you with energy. Proper sleep helps with your cognitive development and progression. I'm no doctor but I do know the plethora of results that come with sleep and that is one aspect of my lifestyle I am grateful for. That, my friend, is priceless.

Being able to manage my own time gives me the opportunity to create the structure I so need. Studies show the importance for children and students to have structure and routine for better performance, but this is also true for adults. I credit my mom and also my educational background that impels me to create routines and systems in my daily life. After eight hours of sleep, I spend quiet time with God every morning. I'm aware of how easy it is for doubt and worry to creep in and attempt to take over my thoughts before I even get out of bed if I'm not mindful. This time allows me to meditate, pray, and get into a grateful mindset. I ask for guidance in whatever area is needed for the day and I always expect good things. I can enjoy my coffee or tea and just be. I am intentional about removing any thoughts that do not align with my peace. Yes, negative thoughts may enter my mind but I am quick to acknowledge them and stop them before they highjack my precious time. Before work, play, or anything else I have to attend to, this quiet time comes first. This is the most important part of my day, without a doubt. I look forward to this time. I yearn for it; I need it.

Even when I'm traveling, my quiet time is a must! I need time to focus on God, otherwise, I have a difficult time taking on the rest of the day. I came to realize the hard way that people seem to wake up and immediately want to talk, eat or get on various devices first thing in the morning. I just can't do it. I've tried when traveling with others and quickly realize how much I depend on that quiet time. My day requires quiet time to be the best me. I guess you could say I'm very stuck in my ways, and yes, I know that can be good and bad. I'm a work in progress.

Being child-free and embracing your freedom does not necessarily go hand in hand. It takes some getting used to, learning how to enjoy you is not as easy as it sounds. A lot of people do not enjoy being alone. They equate alone with lonely and that's just not the case. Learning to not just love yourself but like who you are is a huge life lesson. Having time and the tools as an adult to really understand who you are and how unique your life is, is life changing. Being alone lets the most vulnerable part of you be revealed and when we acknowledge a thing, we can mend a thing. I mean, if you don't like to be alone and spend quality time getting to know yourself, why would anyone else want to?

When a woman decides to become a mother, she is deciding to do away with her personal freedoms, at least temporarily. We all know the real boss of the house is the baby! I'm sure it helps to have two active parents, but even then the baby is running it. Your life becomes consumed with the baby (as it should) because that's part of parenting. Having the option to spend time alone is no longer as accessible. Doing what you want is not an option anymore for most moms as it is for this lifestyle. I don't want to come off insensitive, just want to account for CF living correctly. I admire so many of my family members and friends who chose the sacrifice to be wonderful mothers for their children. I admire the hard work, dedication, and unconditional love it takes. I admire the thankless job women all over the world are doing and doing with grace on a daily. This is why it is so important to be transparent about motherhood and what it takes. Just because you can have a baby doesn't necessarily mean you should. Don't let the instaworld fool you into thinking being a mom is all fun and no work. Fill your cup first, so you can then pour out love, compassion, wisdom, patience and yes, options!

My grandmother and my mom were and are absolutely favored by God with their parenting skills. There are so many wonderful moms out there that go above and beyond to give their children a beautiful life. I could name several great mothers in my life that I look up to and admire but I also know better than to start some mess! There are too many to name and I'm not leaving anybody out! No ma'am.

Do I get bored? Not so much! On most days, I am wishing I had more hours to do the things I set out to do. The freedom I get to experience for the rest of my life as a child-free woman, I do not take lightly. Having the flexibility and privilege to change my schedule at the drop of a dime is not lost on me. The freedom to decide if I want to make a few stops after work or catch a fitness class at the gym (or virtual these days) is priceless. Even something simple like visiting a loved one or meeting a friend for lunch anytime I want is unmatched. The freedom, does it for me. Coming home after a long day to a clean, quiet house is so refreshing and peaceful. I don't think I'll ever get tired of that. I can watch whatever shows I choose when I want and trust me, it is a big deal. If my husband and I decide to take off for a few days and travel, we do just that. I have the pleasure of taking a nap if I choose or curl up and read a good book to relax and unwind. Having freedom and time is just something you can not compare. I don't ever tire from having time. I embrace every day! My husband and I raised our niece from five months old to almost three years old. When I tell you, how those simple, small activities that we may take for granted mean the world when you don't have them. They truly do. I absolutely love my niece and enjoyed watching her grow and learn new things. She definitely made an impact in our lives. All I'm saying is I appreciate my time. I remember watching *Yo Gabba Gabba, Backyardigans, Dora, Barney, Good Night Moon* and every other children's show that was available. I swear I started talking like the characters. It was a lot. We didn't have all the handheld devices everyone uses now, and I most certainly didn't give her my phone. So, yes,

I am definitely grateful for television choice. The perks of being CF should not be criticized or diminished. If we're going to be transparent and have conversations with youth, we want them to know as much as possible to make the best decisions.

Let's not forget the freedom to eat what you want. That may seem silly as well, but when you are limited to what a child will eat, it is something you have to get creative with and it ain't easy. I do not miss eating chicken nuggets, noodles, and bread everyday to be honest. My niece was all about the carbs, lol. It didn't matter how good of a cook I thought I was she was not having it. I probably didn't see vegetables for days on end. My husband and I were blessed to have my parents watch my niece on the weekends so we could actually eat meals we enjoyed or go to restaurants and order adult cuisine. So yes, even the freedom to select your own meal is refreshing. Although, I will say, if I was more aware of baby-led weaning back then, I may had been more successful with mealtime.

The freedom to come and go is another privilege that is not lost on me. The freedom to pack light is a game changer. The freedom to take a long shower is underrated. The freedom to have one, two, three cocktails on a Tuesday night (not a suggestion...I'm just saying) is underestimated. It's natural for us to want what we don't have. Rather than focus on what you don't have, focus on what you do have and all the privileges your child-free life affords you. Change your lonely mentality to embracing your alone time and discover how cool you are to be around.

I'm aware that the child-free lifestyle is not possible for everyone and that's why I consider it a blessing and you should too! Your time, independence, and freedom have been given to you to manipulate the way you see fit, so be thankful for each day. Live in the present. Don't get caught up in the would've, could've, should've. You have today. Live your best life.

We know it's just human nature, thinking the grass is greener on the other side. Well, what we see oftentimes is a mirage of what it really is. If we would stop admiring "their" grass, maybe we could use that same energy to water and tend to our own grass. That's the same idea with freedom. You'll be so preoccupied trying to fill up every minute in your day with "stuff" and what others are doing that you might miss the opportunity to attend to you, until it's gone.

Do I ever wonder what kind of mom I would've been? Do I wonder who will take care of me when I'm old? No, I don't. I really try to focus on being present and not letting my mind wander. Believe me when I say, I overthink enough, there's no need to add more, lol. I'd rather focus on being the best me right now. I prefer to take care of myself today and not worry about *one day*. I am focused on being a loving wife, daughter and friend. Being a great aunt and awesome godmother. Being a supporter. Being a light. Just being. My faith is strong!

CF life has many ups and a few downs but embracing your freedom is definitely all. the. way. up.

Enjoy your time and get to know you. Learn something new, try something new, and think about freedom or time in a different way. Think about how you can make the most of it. Embrace the quietness today (read, write, pray, meditate, stretch, do yoga, listen to an audiobook while lying on your back in the middle of the floor). With social media we do all sorts of challenges. How about accepting the challenge of self love and freedom? Be intentional with your time. There is so much to do and learn about yourself. It's hard for me to get bored. Journaling is a great activity to release your thoughts in a constructive way. Taking a walk/hike is great to get fresh air and enjoy nature. Instead of texting, call a friend or family member. Walk around naked and get to know and love your body. Turn on the music and dance until you sweat or have praise and worship right in your living room. Take a class, something you enjoy like art, poetry, dance, real estate, coding. Don't wait for someone to do it with you or put it off until tomorrow—do it today! Challenge yourself to make each day better than the day before (thanks Joe). Now that's a challenge!

Step 5
ABANDONING GUILT

GUILT HAS ABSOLUTELY been the most challenging feeling to overcome for me. Whether it was guilt from my decision to opt out or guilt from loving my unconventional life too much while others were struggling, I felt guilty. Sometimes it was the guilt of not feeling as though I accomplished enough in my life. I've also experienced spiritual guilt, worrying that what I've chosen may not have been God's plan for me. The guilt from having so much mercy and knowing I didn't deserve it. One way or another, guilt just seemed to follow me and got the best of me on many occassions throughout my life. Everyday, I remind myself that guilt leads to fear and shame. If I don't acknowledge it right away, it will attempt to hold me hostage. That is no longer acceptable for me. The definition of guilt is a feeling of responsibility or remorse for some offense, crime, or wrong-whether it is real or imagined. Wow, I'm sure if you're like me, a lot of what we feel guilty for is either imagined or the story we've created in our mind. So, to be free from guilt and condemnation, we must speak truth and affirm ourselves instead of allowing the guilt to fester. To paraphrase a phenomenal woman, Dr. Maya Angelou, when we know better we can do better.

When I listen to women discuss the issues they go through with their children and grandchildren, oftentimes my heart hurts for them. I know parenting is the hardest job in the world and doesn't come without pain, exhaustion, fear, uncertainty, and yes, guilt! I know parenting is never-ending. Once children are raised and grown, parents look forward to claiming their lives again. Yet, many children come back home with their own children, making them grandparents before they are able to adapt to the new found freedom. In most cases from what I've been told, being a grandmother is one of the greatest gifts and welcomed with open arms. But for some it hits very differently and can be traumatizing for the adult and child. I understand this because I've witnessed it firsthand in my own family and as a teacher. The guilt I feel aslo comes from working in education for so long and observing so many injustices that have to be made right in order to produce a healthier society. Unfortunately, this guilt weighs heavy on me. Again, I must remind myself of who is ultimately in charge and try to stay focused on that. I admit some days are more difficult than others.

I've learned over the years that the guilt I oftentimes felt was actually a feeling of conviction. Conviction comes from a personal relationship with God, it is a healthy part of spirituality. God is not mad at you or getting you back for anything. That feeling helps us to be aware of our flaws and stay humble. Most people assume you have to stop everything you enjoy to be spiritual. The change actually takes place in your heart and in your thinking. I can hear or witness a wrongdoing and in my spirit I have unrest. I will do or say something that I know is wrong and that feeling rises. That unrest feeling used to translate as guilt but now I understand it differently. Guilt makes us feel useless and shameful, which neither are true. We all have things that we regret or wish we could get a do over but if you've learned from it, accept it. When I felt guilt, most likely, I was focused on me and what I cou'd've, should've, would've done and didn't. When I feel convicted for something now I intentionally pause and focus my attention on God's love and forgiveness. I take the opportunity to recognize that I am aware of right and wrong and use it as a time to repent, learn and turn it into a positive. Guilt is by far the most dangerous in my opinion because it has anger, shame and fear twisted in it. Guilt leads a lot of us to blame and when we are consumed with blame we can't forgive. Guilt had to be the hardest feeling for me to overcome.

Just to reiterate, living an intentional life means doing something deliberately and with purpose. It requires thought, planning, and patience. It is NOT allowing life's circumstances to determine your day, week, or future. Not making rash, emotional decisions, which all too often lead to guilt. Some may feel as though they can't be intentional due to the chains they inherited. This untruth leaves one feeling unstable and hopeless. Some were born into situations and circumstances that were out of their control and feel they don't have choices. I get it and it's not right, which is why taking time to incorporate healthy proactive tools is so crucial. Yes it may be that much harder for you to break your cycle but it is no less achievable. Beating yourself up and criticizing yourself will only lead to more guilt and of course, shame. The same kind words you would offer to a friend who messed up, offer to yourself. I know it is not the easiest thing to do, but again, be intentional and consistent about it. Like anything that involves change, it becomes more manageable day by day. When you truly gain control over your emotions, you can take back your life. People who lack this control feel like they are on an emotional roller coaster. One day they are happy and feeling great and the next day they are sad and feeling depressed. That same person may feel like they are on top of the world because someone gave them a compliment or a "like." But the next minute they are full of rage and feeling invisible because they didn't get what they were looking for. Having bad days because bad energy has been let into their mind space. A constant state of feeling high then feeling low, relying on external influences to guide your day. From one extreme to the next, depending on how others treat you. Giving people the power to dictate your emotions has to be dealt with deliberately. Remind yourself, they do not deserve that power over you. That's why knowing who you are is so important to your mental health. Being tuned in and changing what you think about is key. Harboring feelings of guilt is a sure way to self destruction. The ability to stop and ask God for help and guidance rather than allow thoughts or circumstances to determine your next move is a huge step in the right direction. Inhale....We have to be willing to do it differently. Let go of guilt controlling everything and let God. Exhale...

Oh yes, guilt can be relentless. There was a time in my life when I would feel guilty just talking to mothers. Not wanting to sound insensitive or crass with my freedom and lack of responsibility (as far as children are concerned). I was always filtering my thoughts mid conversation to avoid offending someone. Which is another reason why I feel my unique sisters need to have support. It's nice to express yourself without internalizing every comment.

More guilt came from not meeting everyone else's expectations. Family members relying on you to continue their lineage. Guilt, that I let people down. That I somehow cheated and did not have to endure the physical scars that come from childbirth. I mean guilt has met me at every turn! Blaming myself for not having and then blame from having too much. Guilt for my many actions that do not always align with the word. And just when it feels like I'm going to lose it again, I remembered to pause, breathe, and pray. And, for me that always puts things into perspective and gives me the opportunity to get out of my head and stay present.

Yes, there is a place and time for guilt. As we grow and develop, guilt helps us to acknowledge right from wrong and learn our moral compass. It's funny how guilt changes from helping us to hurting us, or better yet, hurting ourselves. Having so many unnecessary expectations will do it every time. If I feel like my husband and I are enjoying our lives too much, it can bring guilt. It's as though we have been wired to work, work, work and stay busy so much that I feel guilt when I'm relaxing and enjoying life. Which is another standard or expectation Americans try to live up to. Spend all your time working or being busy; the term workaholic is used almost like a badge of honor. Unless, you are wealthy or part of the elite, you should not fully enjoy life. These examples may sound trivial but for someone like myself who lives with so much empathy, it can be hard to enjoy what you have because you're always thinking about others who don't or have less than. This guilt like all guilt came from ME overthinking and self-condemnation and not focusing on God's blessings. Having time and freedom is amazing, but again, I have to be intentional. Over the years I have learned to forgive and abandon my guilt. Less of me and more of You, is a constant prayer.

The guilt is not limited to internal guilt, sometimes it comes from external sources. For example, while having a discussion with one of my aunts, we wondered why so many people insist on recognizing child-free women on Mother's Day. Is it just an automatic response or does it come from guilt? Do they wish we were mothers? Do they think this is a compliment somehow? This subject is one I never quite understood. When I'm out and about and a stranger wishes me a happy Mother's Day because it happens to be, is odd, but it happens. A lot. Again, society just assumes if you're a woman, you must be a mom. But when it comes from friends and family members who are well aware of my status and still feel the need to get me a card or send a text ,

I'm puzzled. I guess I've gotten used to it. I would love to just honor them and not have them feel the need to say it back when it's not my day. I'm cool with the day being theirs.

Even when our response is, "Oh, I'm not a mother," it is almost always met with, "But you're a mother figure" or "You're a mother to your puppies." Well, no disrespect and I hope my friends and family don't take this the wrong way but by mother figure, do you mean aunt or godmother or teacher? I am most definitely all those things and my dogs' favorite person, I might add but I am not a mother. I guess after many years of attempting to correct people, I just decided to leave it be. But I actually hope it will change for those coming up behind me. I (we), in no way feel the need to be told Happy Mother's Day. It doesn't make us feel good or validated at all. How about we we just have a National Auntie's Day or Godmother's Day and you can tell us then and buy us all the gifts your heart desires. Being a mother is so valuable that I (we) don't want to take that credit. I don't need to add stealing your day to my guilt list! But for real, jokes aside, keep that day for yourself please. You deserve it!

When my husband and I stepped in to help raise my niece, we were being great siblings to my sister. And quite possibly the best aunt and uncle ever, lol! I still didn't want Mother's Day cards. In addition to that,

I was able to experience day-to-day duties of mother-hood without being a mother. I believe God used this situation to answer my prayers and to confirm our decision not to have children. God moves in mysterious ways. And I don't mean that in a flippant way at all. I know this was a blessing for us, my sister, and my niece. Now, there are women out there who are raising family members permanently and have every right to think differently. From my viewpoint and other CF perspectives, we don't want Mother's Day cards, simply because we don't do what mothers do. We do not sacrifice what mothers sacrifice. So, please take this with love: Go ahead and celebrate mothers without including your child-free friends and family. I hope I am freeing you as much as it is freeing to me. We want to celebrate you, especially on Mother's Day. Enjoy it!

We may not be able to get rid of guilt entirely but we can start with forgiveness. You can free yourself rather than beat yourself up. It took me awhile to truly begin to forgive myself, not just for one thing in particular but ongoing forgiveness. Daily forgiveness. Waking up every day and believing I am the righteousness of God. Knowing that I'm flawed and it's okay. Knowing that nothing I do will make God stop loving me. Total forgiveness.

It takes daily effort to stay sane. I know that might sound dramatic but for me, it is real. Usually I come off pretty calm, cool and collected. Partly because of my DNA (my dad definitely gave me that gene). But I believe it's mostly from the daily effort I put into being present and knowing who I am spiritually. Knowing and hearing that God is all forgiving and died so we can receive it is one thing. Believing and being willing to put your faith (whatever amount of faith you come with) in something bigger and greater than you takes work not weakness. We are human and can only see life from our limited viewpoint. If we just trust our physical eyes, family history, and experiences, we are stuck in our ordinary lives. When we let go of past trauma or how we've been living and just let God, He will show us unprecedented living.

Guilt may never go away but conviction we should hope doesn't go away either. At least for me, that reminds me of *whose* I am. Dare to have faith. Try putting your trust in something greater than yourself. People believe in karma, fate, horoscopes, but refuse to believe in God, in Jesus. You may feel like you are betraying people or yourself, just take a risk. You may think you are too set in your ways to ever change. You may try it for a week and think, "This is ridiculous!" You may even believe the bible is a fictional book made up of stories and myths. But when is the last time you tried something that would guarantee to make your life better, fuller, richer, healthier, and more at peace and you regretted it? I'll wait . . .

People will try all sorts of diets, pills, surgeries, get

rich quick schemes, and many other things that promise satisfaction but don't truly add to the quality of their life. But aren't willing to allow themselves to get uncomfortable to do the daily work for real fulfillment. Being uncomfortable is not a bad thing. You need to be uncomfortable to grow. No one said it would be easy, no matter what lifestyle we choose. The goal isn't to have it easy; the goal is to do it with grace and to live a life that is bigger than your physical body. We are not our bodies; we are not limited to what our bodies do or don't do. We are so much more.

"Truly he is my rock and my salvation, He is my fortress, I shall never be shaken."
-Psalms 62:1-2

Step 6

ACCEPTING YOUR GIFTS

SONG
"GOD IN ME"
MARY MARY

YES, YOU ARE so much more. You don't have to dim your light or silence your voice because it doesn't fit the typical mold. I hope you now believe it is not necessary to live up to superficial standards just because everyone else is chasing the so-called American dream. Be authentically you. You are wonderfully and fearfully made. Too many people are trying to keep up with the Joneses for social status, so much, that we don't even know what is real anymore. It's all about comparing and competing. Social media is definitely a contributor to the insecurities and comparisons that already exist, especially with our youth. They are so easily influenced and quick to attach themselves to the hottest whatever! There is so much noise in the world telling them who they are supposed to be, what they should look like, how to feel and even what to think. So much that a lot of young people are confused about who they are. They have been raised by technology and fantasy, that many don't realize their own gifts and dreams. They try so hard to keep up with all the latest and they start believing the lies. Well, I say instead of keeping up with the Joneses be the Joneses, the Fords (of course I did) or whomever you are called to be! Who has time to be keeping up with everybody else? Why waste your precious energy chasing their dreams?

So back to the idea that being fruitful goes beyond the womb. Being child-free does not negate being fruitful by any means. The ability to birth dreams, ideas, nations, change and birth generational wealth is a huge undertaking. Being fruitful has more to do with using your gifts to enrich and cultivate. Being fruitful is just as much about giving and thriving than reproducing. You can still have life and life abundantly when you use your gift(s) to light the path for others. Having children is one way to multiply certainly not the only. Innovators start out with dreams, passions and gifts to change the world beyond themselves. So remember this next time someone tells you, you were created to be fruitful and multiply. Correct! We can agree on that.

Our gifts come in many shapes, sizes, and voices and they all can be used. We have gifts and talents that are innate. Our responsibility is to realize them, develop them and share them. Whether it is perfecting your craft on your own or going to school to attain a degree or license in a particular field, you can use your platform to empower. When thinking of a gift or talent, it is typically something that comes easy for you.Something that you enjoy and have a desire to do. There are those who know what this is at a young age and for some these gifts have to be discovered over time. Some of us have so many layers to break through before we realize or can even submit to our gifts. Sometimes our gifts are not as glamorous as we were hoping they'd be. Being in denial is common because we want our gift to look like someone else's gift. It may take being patient with yourself. Timing is a huge factor. Get to know who you really are, without getting it confused with what you have to do to make ends meet. Jobs and gifts are not always identical.

Frequently people consider gifts and purpose to be synonymous. On my journey for understanding, I have come to recognize that gifts are personal to each and every one of us. Purpose, in my humble opinion, is more collective. We all have the same purpose for being on this earth. That purpose is to love, honor, and serve one another. A lot of us spend so much time trying to figure out our purpose in life. Waiting for God to show us our purpose. He showed us with his life. He was kind, loved the unlovable, and used his life to bless others. That is our purpose, plain and simple. I do not believe understanding life's purpose was intended to be complicated or a mystery. We are all God's children and we all have the responsibility to love and help our brothers and sisters in whatever way we can. Now, the way you show up, love, and give back is your personal gift(s). Teaching, for me, is my most dominate gift I would say. Teaching is not only something I do, it's who I am. I have always found it gratifying to plant seeds and empower the young minds of so many students I've been blessed to work with.

Being a teacher is very natural for me. Yes, I consider it a gift but I'm sure the influence also came from my mother who would teach her sixth grade students, as I laid napping behind her desk when I was a little girl.

I knew it was a profession that was greatly undervalued and still, I chose to serve. I can only imagine how many people have changed their opinions of teachers after the year we all experienced in 2020.

I have always been more interested in pursuing what I'am called to do rather than the money I can make. Staying true to myself sometimes meant going against the grain. Sometimes it meant being overlooked because my title wasn't fancy enough. Other times it meant, standing up for myself when others passed judgement. Meaningful work surpasses monetary worth for me hands down. If your gift or passion brings you both, well that's a win, win!

I don't know who needs to hear this but you do not have to change what you are passionate about because other people don't understand it. If your gift doesn't come wrapped in a shiny box, it is no less valuable. Trying to get approval from others is too exhausting. I just can't do it. If you are constantly changing to appease someone and feel the need to modify your gift, most likely they are not a friend or someone who wants the best for you. They may be a follower or an admirer, but there is a difference. Pay attention. It shows up in the interactions, the conversations, and the expectations from a person. I am learning to trust my instinct. What is for me, is for me. Motives are so important. Spoiler alert: Everyone you meet does not have your best interest at heart. Sometimes less is better. We have to learn to trust the process and know that everything we may want to do is not necessarily a gift.

Although I knew teaching wouldn't make me rich, seeing my paycheck for the first year was heart breaking and humbling. I quickly realized, I wouldn't be living the lifestyle some of my peers (whether they graduated from college or not) talked about. I struggled at times, but I was always able to find the silver lining in my situation and enjoy my "broke life." It may have looked like I was *settling* to some, but I'm just not built to keep up with the world. I knew God was faithful and I didn't worry about what I couldn't afford. When others were vacationing all around the world and buying all the name brand bags and shoes, I've always been content with what I had. Finding my entire life in Ross has always been easy for me. Not to mention, my mom enjoys shopping and always seems to find things just my size (she appreciates name brands more than I do). It doesn't matter how old I get, she won't stop. So I'm sure people think all I do is shop for clothes, LOL, I so don't. I'm a DIY kind of lady, from my own hair to manicures and pedis. I have always taken the time to get myself right together right at home if need be. And guess what? I was absolutely okay with it. It wasn't that I didn't dream or aspire to have more but I knew my time would come. Being patient, having a grateful heart, and prayer, changes things! Now, if I want to pamper myself or pay to get my hair done, it's my choice.

Although my life was good, there were times when I wondered if I was making the right decisions. I wondered why my gift paid so little. And yes I questioned if I could get to a place where I would be totally content. But through prayer, faith and grace any doubt about my purpose and gifts have been removed. I am confident in who I've become. The peace that passes all understanding has to be God.

Another gift I have is the gift of listening. I know that sounds comical, but everyone does not listen. They may hear you, but not listen. It is definitely a great quality to have as a teacher and I believe it is a gift as well. Sometimes listening is the greatest gift. Listening to my grandparents tell stories. Listening to a child read, especially after they've struggled for so long. Listening to an inspiring message. Listening to the word. Sometimes we just need to listen. You can be a saving grace to someone by simply listening. The older I get, the more I appreciate listening. Yes, when we're in those early decades of life, most of us think we have all the answers but there will come a time when you realize you don't and the best thing to do is listen.

Now, in no way am I suggesting you become someone's therapist or feel a responsibility to listen to all their drama and mess. That's what professionals are for. Being a listener also comes with boundaries. There's a difference with allowing someone to vent in a respectful, healthy way as oppose to verbally throwing up on you every time you talk to a particular person. Someone who speaks negatively or complains all the time is like being verbally assaulted. By the time you get off of the phone or leave that person's presence, you feel drained! That's not healthy and not at all what I mean by being a listener. It took some time to figure that out because people will take advantage of even the gift of listening if you let them. Be protective of what you have, boundaries are a must. Speaking can also be a gift. Singing, healing, creating, building, leading, and the gift list goes on and on. There are many gifts we're given. You owe it to yourself to uncover what you have inside of you and not try to duplicate someone else's. There's enough space for all of us to co-exist with our unique gifts. Trust me when I tell you that it is so freeing when you have confidence in knowing you are living your best life without the pressures of measuring up. I am selective of who I share my personal space with because I've learned that my peace means more to me than an opinion.

Outside of my spiritual relationship, the most critical relationship I have is with myself and it has been a scenic journey, let me tell you, to reach my authentic self. I enjoy my relationship with me more and more. I love my blessed life and wouldn't trade it for anything in the world. As much as I admire Oprah, Michelle, Beyonce' and many others, I understand our gifts look different. I am a fan but I respect their gifts and I accept mine. No matter who you are, your gift is just as powerful. It's our gifts that make us one of a kind. So it's okay to be inspired by someone but wanting their life and feeling the need to emulate them will not end well for you. Put that energy into finding your uniqueness. And that's the truth!

Being an educator is a gift that keeps on giving. I

know that I have the opportunity to plant seeds into so many brilliant minds. As teachers, we know that we may not always see end result, but we can be confident in knowing what we planted will bloom one day! I am aware that my gift(s) are not for me alone. Gifts are given to us so that we can elevate others. They are so much bigger than you and I. Once you understand the true meaning of your gifts, you will be able to focus on meaningful relationships, prioritize what's important and ignore all the distractions that are constantly dominating your mind.

Therefore, there isn't a day that goes by that I am not happy, thankful, and passionate about what I do. Even in the midst of a hard day at work, I feel honored to be a teacher. Teaching is a career that cannot be taught…oxymoron, right? I strongly believe that it can be developed but not taught. If it isn't in you to be compassionate, empowering and patient, it is not for you. There is also a quality that I can't quite put into words but great teachers know it and have it. Just because you graduated with a teaching degree doesn't necessarily mean you are effective at it. Being a teacher really comes from a special place and if you don't have it in your heart and soul then do the kids and yourself a favor and get out! It's not fair to the children if your heart is not in it or if you thought you were signing up for an easy career with lots of breaks. WRONG! I'm just saying! You'd probably be great at something else without breaking a child's spirit. It is so important to examine your motives. Teaching is not an easy job, they just pay us like it is. And now, to add virtual learning and teaching to the mix....Lord, help us all! Just like parenting, teaching is also not for everyone.

As I said before, I knew teaching wouldn't make me rich financially but rich in other areas of my life. And look at God, He also made sure I would be financially comfortable today. Thank you God for my life!

Your dominant gift may not be your only gift. But you may be unable to recognize your gift(s) if you are carrying guilt, shame, and judgement from your past. Be patient and allow yourself to be vulnerable. What you uncover may be painful but it is a chance to keep healing. Unmask it all, you may be surprised by who you truly are. You just might love her!

Outside of teaching, I always wondered what it would be like to be a chef. I am intrigued by culinary artists. I mean, I enjoy cooking and I enjoy eating even more. I consider myself a foodie, for sure! Which is why I try to be diligent about working out. I want to eat what I want, when I want! I often watch the cooking shows and imagine myself on television. I do think cooking is a gift for some just not necessarily my gift. Like a lot of people, I just happen to think I'm good at it. I might not be able to make everything but I have my specialties. I like to recreate meals I've had but put my own twist on them. My husband has even brought home mystery bags with random items and asked, "What can you make from this?" And off I go taking my mystery ingredients and whipping up something delicious. He just loves my food creations. We watch a little too much Food Network, I know.

Every week, I look forward to grocery shopping and planning meals. At least I did before March 2020, of course, when I could take my time and get lost in the aisles. I would rather go grocery shopping than any other type of shopping. My mind just goes wild when I'm in a grocery store. I feel right at home. Trust me, I'm aware that most people do not find pleasure in grocery shopping but again, I realize that I am not like most people. Cooking allows me to be creative, control what I put in my body, and is very rewarding.

These days, COVID has taken going to the grocery store and restaurants to a whole new level. I am masked up, wiped down, and in and out like nobody's business.

Now, I realize most people use the term *talents*. Someone may be considered a talented athlete or dancer because of what they are physically capable of, but I feel that can be limiting. I prefer to spotlight what is inside of you. Gifts may not be seen but they can be felt.

Accepting or embracing your gifts and purpose in life as a child-free woman is so attainable. Being true to yourself and believing you are good enough will give you power. That power will fuel you to take ownership of your life and release blaming others. This puts you in a position to not fear the unknown but embrace it. Accomplishing something that you once doubted will give you confidence. Building your confidence may take time but with every achievement (big or small) it increases. When you allow others to control your actions or your destiny your confidence will decrease. Know your worth without anyone's approval. The world doesn't define your identity. Placing your identity on what you're attached to is never a good idea. Children will grow and leave at some point. Spouses or partners may leave or pass at some point. Just know who you are without anyone affirming that for you and know that you can do all things. Some women truly believe their purpose in life is to be a mother and I won't argue that. I just hope they also feel and know that their children *reflect* them not *define* them. Know that your worth is not dependent on people or babies. Be good with you and discover the gifts you've been given to add joy and excitement to your life. Let anything that you "birth" or do be an addition to who you are, not the whole story. Know that you are worth it!

Whether you know what your gifts are or still discovering, the more time you take learning yourself the easier you can identify your strengths. Be willing to try different things. Be willing to ask for help. Be willing to talk to God and listen.

Be intentional. Live on purpose and your special gifts will be unveiled.

There are many routes and paths that lead to the same destination. The different gifts that make our lives fruitful, map out our private and exclusive journey. When in doubt, just keeping going. We may not have all the answers when we want them but you can still enjoy the ride. God gave us the free will to make our own decisions as long as we also humble ourselves, honor Him and lift one another up..

"Empowered people are not concerned about competing with anyone; They are busy empowering others.
                    —Rhonda Hendricks

Step 7
FINDING PEACE

SONG
"GOTTA FIND PEACE OF MIND"
LAURYN HILL

AFTER ALL THIS, you may still ask, "When will I find peace?" or "How will I know if I have it?" Well, I'm not going to pretend that I have all the answers or say something specific is going to happen when you have it. You won't wake up one day and claim that it's the day you finally have all your ish together! That's just not how life works. I spend many days visiting with my grandparents and I'm assured that even at their season in life, they continue to be amazed at what God can do. You don't ever feel like you made it and life is perfect and perhaps that's not even the goal. The peace comes somewhere in the process of learning, trusting and believing. The more time and effort you dedicate to your spiritual self, the more natural it becomes. You will come to a place where you have calmness and serenity when all around you is chaos. You can rest and know you are living out your purpose. It's like there's an ease about your life that you can't explain but you know it's happening. But don't mistake ease for easy.

Finding your peace takes time and is ongoing. Some days are better than others but like I've said before, even on the "other" days you can still be grateful and have a calmness that passes understanding. Some days we can't find our peace because we are too busy with distractions. We fill our days with meetings, events, deadlines and dilemmas. Not to mention, the ever present social media. Being busy is not a sign of success. Sometimes being busy can be a peace stealer. Yes, some of our jobs are more demanding than others, true! Some of us have more energy than others, very true! But when being busy compromises your health—mental, physical or spiritual—it can't be worth it! Slowing down to let your mind rest is so necessary. I have repeatedly suggested that you breathe. The power of intentional breathing is highly underrated. Breathe and learn to listen to your body or the still voice of reason speaking from within. Breathe and feel your body release tension and anxiety. If you don't feel it, keep breathing—by now you can inhale through your nose for seven seconds (hold it), and out for seven. And repeat. Every. Day. Breathe. Thoughtfully.

Peace is something you have to really fight for. Our minds are constantly under attack with so much clutter, it's no surprise that so many people are on medication just to silence the noise. When you are under the impression that the more you do, the busier your day is and the less you relax amounts to productivity, you have missed it. That is so far from the truth. Be mindful and recognize the difference between meaningful work and empty tasks that may be compromising your peace. If something is costing you your peace or you can not turn the noise off, you owe it to yourself to carve out some quiet time to focus and of course breathe.

In no way is my journey over. I am forty-eight years old and still in awe almost daily. For years, I would write in my journals, but in no way, shape, or form did I think I was qualified to write a book. And quite frankly, I still don't think I am. I didn't have a team of experts to correct my grammar or fine-tune everything. I just knew I had something to say. I tried ignoring the crazy idea until I decided it was time to just step out on faith and do it. I had to conquer the fear of not having a deep enough story or traumatic enough heartache to write about. Like most of us, I've had my share of trauma but my journey is not defined by trauma alone. The fear of people not understanding my perspective blocked me on many occassions. Then I was reminded that we all have something to give. Even our unique journeys can help someone. I had to remember exactly what I've told you. We are ALL a part of the same purpose and if my life can uplift, speak to, or empower one person, it was worth it!

The peace I have in my life now does not allow me to be afraid of what people will say or think. The peace I have gained over time is such a part of my life that I had to write this book just to celebrate me in my own way. I want child-free women to know their value and worth. I want my nieces, cousins, and girls everywhere to know they have options. I need them to know that no matter what others may say or do, having a fulfilled life is absolutely accessible without having children or getting married.

Prioritizing my peace has forced me to reflect on all the things I can control in my life. I hope I never stop discovering and learning. I really do want to learn something new, every day.

My peace comes from my faith and my willingness to change my thinking as often as needed. Doubt, insecurities, and negative thinking will always show up but I have learned that I have authority over my thoughts. I've learned that being selfish is not always a bad thing. I have learned that you can't please everybody but you can please God. I may never have all the answers and I'm cool with that. I'm at a place where the unknown is tolerable because my anchor is steadfast.

What I do know is that I have peace. There is a comfort and knowing in my spirit that I am content with no matter the day or situation. I think being in quarantine throughout this COVID pandemic has made that even more clear for me. In an odd way, 2020 has given me better vision. I have always been reflective and very much an introvert—not to be mistaken for timid or scared. But being forced to stay in, sit down, and think was a whole different type of obedience. My husband and I have never spent so much time together, like I'm sure most of you can attest to. I've learned to appreciate him even more since he has proven he can deal with me 24/7 and still want to cuddle every night. It was not only beneficial to my spiritual growth but my mental growth as well. 2020 granted me the space to close certain chapters in my life and not feel guilty about it. Some people are in our lives for a season and their purpose comes to an end. If someone is mentally draining or not serving a positive purpose in your life, it is time to move on.

When forming relationships, have an open mind and an open heart. I believe this lesson comes with age and is so important. No, it's not always easy, so you really have to be intentional. If I can help the next person I absolutely will. I am eager to support new businesses and celebrate victories, especially for women. Helping and supporting others brings joy to your life that you can only experience by doing. Some people will only lend a helping hand if there's something in it for them. Well, life has a funny way of teaching you that what you do for others is not always reciprocated. Expecting others to treat you the way you treat them sounds fair but in reality, doesn't happen often. That's why it is so critical to know your worth. No matter how good you are to someone, they may never show gratitude. Don't let their bitterness shift your focus. Stay the course and keep shining your light. When you learn that hard life lesson, supporting and being there for others also brings peace. God will bless your life when you bless others. Having a pure heart and doing something because it's the right thing to do and not for recognition is the ultimate blessing. Another lesson I'm learning is to not take things so personally. Usually, it's not about you, it's about them. Not taking things personally I know is difficult, especially when you feel attacked but do it for yourself, your peace of mind is worth it. I am learning to show more grace. People are just people, we all have issues. Some just have more hurt, fear and brokenness than others. It's important to remind yourself of that often, because those are the little insignificant things that will steal your peace and have you overthinking for no good reason. Peace can easily be highjacked if we're not careful. I can't stress enough how everyday activities can steal your peace and before you know it, you are consumed with negative thoughts and fear.

It is human nature for us to want validation but knowing what type of validation will sustain you is key. Extrinsic validation may bring temporary peace but it won't last. But investing in true peace gives you stability, stamina, and restores your soul. Peace is internal and very personal. When you are genuine about what you're doing, it brings peace. Joyce Meyers once said, "It's very easy sometimes for us to deceive ourselves about our motives—the 'why' behind the 'what'—so it's good to take the time occasionally to ask God to show us anything that we might be doing for a wrong reason." In education, we write objectives stating the *how* for every *what*. The standard being taught is the what and the way your students show their comprehension is the *how*. In life we must understand our "why" to ensure our hearts are in the right place. Motives are critical when seeking peace.

I don't mean to harp on social media but since it is the primary mode these days, it has to be reiterated. It is so unhealthy on many levels. For one, it has replaced real interaction and communication for so many people, especially the young community. It compromises our eyes, neck, and too often, puts us in a negative mind space. Now of course I understand the benefits of technology and social media and I am extremely thankful for those things. But like I mentioned in Step four, anything in excess can be harmful. The more social media dependent we are, the less peace we will have. It's impossible to gain peace from things that are always changing; hot today, gone tomorrow. Comments that offend you or not getting enough likes, can be all-consuming and strip away your peace without you even realizing it. It's sad to me that we have become social media fiends. Our every waking minute seems to be device dependent. I know this is the 21st century and I'm trying really hard to get with it, LOL. My nieces help to keep me current but social media has changed life forever. If we thought we dealt with pressure, kids today have a heightened sense of judgement, pressure, and stress they carry around daily. Which is why it is so important to me to change the expectations early on and hopefully lay a spiritual foundation that will sustain them. We have to give them other things to think about and lean on besides social media. Even young girls must understand how to honor and value their God given peace, especially now. I do post on social media but I try my best to make it more of a small extension of me and not necessarily a full reflection of my life, if that makes sense. No one needs to know everything!

I think to know me is to interact with me and spend time with me in real life, not social media life. I say that because so many people really treat social media as if it is life! It is so dangerous. Although times have changed and young people feel more connected using social media, research states that it cannot replace physical interaction. Meaningful relationships never get old! Get to know real people. Whether that's working together, developing friendships, or even just the people you meet from day to day—establish real relationships. Be brave and interact in person. Have conversations. That's how I judge a person's character, not by social media. I pray that my real life is more powerful than my posts on any given day. I pray that my life reflects peace in person not just on social media. We all know that social media is just a false sense of reality for most. We have to be careful not to base our lives on what we see and hear, instead find true peace from within. Like the saying goes, social media is the "highlight reel" of what people want you to see, yet you compare it to your backstage, behind-the-scenes actual life. Think about it, it's so true. We just have to be mindful of who we are and whose we are, and be confident in that. That's when you can nurture peace of mind.

Strive to be that peace. When you are in someone's company, they will feel your joy and your peace and know it is genuine. I want people to leave me feeling encouraged and empowered. I want my light to shine in real life. I want to be a reflection of Him!

Conclusion

On this journey we call life, everyone wants to be validated, feel as though their life matters. My hope is that this book affords me the opportunity to empower someone to put in the work and uncover your unmatched value. My desire is to shine my light and touch lives that have not been illuminated on the big screen, highlighted in best selling novels or talked about with enthusiasm and aspiration. We have to initiate our own conversation that will not only normalize but celebrate diverse lifestyles.

The steps in this book are not limited to Child Free living. I believe the tools are beneficial to anybody desiring change and wanting to elevate their life. The steps I have offered do not have to begin and end in a particular order. Think of them as a sphere. Continual effort and repetition has to be implemented. It is ongoing practice. It starts with renewing your mind and in doing so, accepting the truth about who you are and whose you are. Intentionality and consistency better equip you to deal with the numerous feelings and emotions that come with being present and tuned in. Examining these reoccurring feelings is essential in developing ways to control your reaction and attain real healing.

Letting go of what people think and say is a game changer. No, it won't happen instantaneously but it will slowly diminish. When you are no longer moved by folks' opinions, you can bring your focus inward and learn to turn the volume of the world off. Everything does not deserve your attention. Make it a priority to protect your peace at all cost.

I intentionally added -ing to the action words I chose as my chapter titles making them all present participles; Renewing rather than renew, releasing rather than release. This suggest that the process is ongoing, currently happening. All the steps are about daily work and being aware of your thinking. If we change a thought in our mind one time, that thought does not automatically disappear forever. We're human, so good and bad thoughts incessantly pop in and out of our head. It is only by changing that thought over and over again, that you will begin to notice a different mindset. Eventually, your renewed speaking, thinking, and actions become automatic, or at least, a lot more natural to you. You can look at your life as the privilege it is and develop such a grateful heart. It is pretty hard to be grateful and full of anger or fear, at the same time. When you believe how much God loves you, despite knowing everything about you- abandoning that guilt will seem so possible.

This new space in your life will lend itself to understanding your purpose and accepting your internal gift(s).

Your child-free journey or any journey may never make complete sense. Just know that it is setting you up for a time such as this. Preparing you to Shine your Light and dare to be different.

Unspeakable joy and peace that passes all understanding are waiting at the next rest stop. But until you arrive, turn up the music and enjoy the scenery. Remember, you have been given the V.I.P (very individualized path) treatment that few are privy to. Live it unapologetically! Let's create a new meaning for what success looks like. A new mindset for what fruitful can be. New expectations. A new normal!

I hope this book has been inspiring. I hope this book can be the vehicle that helps someone discover the power they have within. Now go let your Light brighten up the pathway for someone else. Enjoy your journey. With Love.

Here's a suggestion that can help bring peace to your life. Try developing a different mindset for each day of the week:

- **Sustaining Sunday:** You might attend church, go for a hike, or meditate. Do something that fills your soul (aka tank) with positive, sustaining fuel. In order To travel this journey called life with grace, you must stay fueled up and fed to endure. Supportive pit crews are essential. Find your like-minded tribe, we're here!

- **Mindful Monday:** Be mindful of your thoughts, words, and actions. Be mindful of your breathing. Make your actions meaningful. Be kind!

- **Tuned-in Tuesday:** From the moment you wake up give thanks for the amazing and terrific Tuesday that is about to unfold. Even if something tries to tell you otherwise, like stubbing your toe on the way to the bathroom or someone gives you upsetting news first thing in the morning, pause and tune in. Remember that you are in control of your reaction. Turn off the noise and tune in to that quiet voice. Take a minute to breathe. Let nothing steal your peace!

- **Whimsical Wednesday:** Life is not all serious.

Make it a point to laugh, be carefree and enjoy the simple things. Do something fun! Bring light and cheerful energy wherever you go. You may be having a difficult day but think of the silver lining. Remind yourself of your blessings and smile. Like Kirk Franklin said, "You look so much better when you smile." Enjoy your life today and don't wait until it's perfect.

- **Thriving Thursday:** It's not enough to just live. Live Your Best Life! Whatever it is that you have been gifted—thrive in it. Make others want to thrive as well. Be contagious with it. Empower others to flourish when they are around you!

- **Freedom Friday:** Free yourself from guilt, shame, fear, and anger. If you don't they will turn into stress and sickness. Live like you have permission to do whatever it is you want. Be intentional about removing the stress. Be free!

- **Serving Saturday:** Whether it is great or small, find a way to be of service to someone outside of your home. Spread love!

I pray that each of you who took the time to read my humble memoir is blessed beyond measure. Thank you from the bottom of my heart.

Essential Questions

CHAPTER 1: RENEWING YOUR MIND

1. Do you think about what you're thinking about? (Metacognition)
2. Can you renew your mind alone?
3. Describe a situation where you intentionally changed your mind/view of something or someone.
4. Is renewing the mind spiritual?

CHAPTER 2: EXAMINING YOUR FEELINGS

1. Name the feeling(s)/emotion(s) that dominate most of your day.
2. How do you feel at this moment? Do you feel in control?
3. What causes you to feel happy or content?

Does it involve someone else?

4. Does what you hear and see affect your feelings?
5. What strategies do you use to control your emotions?

Chapter 3: Releasing Judgement

1. Have you ever been misjudged? How did it make you feel?
2. Who do you feel most judgement from?
3. Do other's opinions matter to you? Why or why not?
4. Do you believe what God says about you?

Chapter 4: Embracing Your Freedom

1. How do you typically spend a day?
2. Are you more of a (routine/structured) or (spontaneous/ in the moment) type of person?
3. Do you speak positively to yourself everyday?
4. Are you comfortable being alone?

Chapter 5: Abandoning Guilt

1. What is something you've felt guilty about? Were you able to forgive yourself?
2. Has someone else made you feel guilty for their actions? Were you able to forgive them?
3. Do you believe God has forgiven you?

Chapter 6: Accepting Your Gifts

1. What do you enjoy doing?
2. What are you good at?
3. What are some traits about yourself that you are proud of?
4. Do you like where your life is at currently? How could it be better?

Chapter 7: Finding Your Peace

1. Would you describe your life as peaceful? Why or why not?
2. Does your internal being (spirit/soul) align with your external (flesh)?
3. On a scale 1-10, how much do you like who you are?
4. How often do you spend intentional quiet time alone?

FUN FACTS

Song
"Just Fine"
Mary J. Blige

1. I have to begin each day with gratitude, prayer, and coffee (okay, maybe you do know this by now).
2. I love to read (mostly autobiographies).
3. I used to write letters to my mom when I was young to express my feelings.
4. When we got married in Vegas, we made a debut on the Food Network Channel.
5. I believe dogs are very spiritual (I mean, dog spelled backwards is god).
6. A good workout makes me feel empowered and sexy (hiking, dancing, swimming, cycling, I like to mix it up).

7. I love spending time with my large family (there's always something going on).
8. I donate regularly (it feels good and reduces my clutter at the same time).
9. I played piano for 8 years.
10. Red wine is my beverage of choice (don't judge).
11. I'll pretty much eat anything cheesy!
12. Switching up my hair gives me life (shout out to all the hair chameleons)!
13. I love traveling with my husband.
14. I have spontaneous jam sessions in my backyard (it's therapeutic).
15. I love making my mom laugh (the laugh that makes you teary eyed).
16. I'm always down for a girl's trip (nothin' like hanging with the ladies).
17. An occassional day of pampering (from head to toe) is like pressing the reset button.
18. I have the best nephews and nieces!
19. I watch too much reality TV (SMDH).
20. My grandparents are my everything!

DESCRIPTION

WOMEN ALL AROUND the world are wrestling with the idea of whether or not they want to have children. Becoming a mother is not an automatic yes for all. The women who decide to opt out are often viewed as less than or unjustly labeled selfish by mainstream society. So many women are made to feel guilty or bad about this decision. Well, I'm here to share my perspective on child-free living. Trust me, you CAN have a beautiful life with purpose and not be a mom! This book will help you learn to:

- Own your decision of being child-free
- Release judgement from yourself and others
- Embrace your freedom and independence
- Abandon your guilt
- Live your best life in peace

You deserve to live a happy life, no matter the route you decide to take. Child-free living is an option to assumed mother/fatherhood. Don't wait for others to decide your future; grab your copy and call your own shots. By the end of this book, you will have the tools to live a fulfilled life even if you never get married, forego motherhood, or do not live up to the copious amount of "standards and expectations" we call the American dream. A full, purposeful life is within your reach!!

ABOUT THE AUTHOR

AFTER STRUGGLING WITH the acceptance to live child-free herself, Lesley Ford now empowers others to live their best life unapologetically with steps that will lead you to self-discovery and confidence from within. Lesley earned a Bachelor's degree in elementary education from Arizona State University. She also holds a Master's degree from Northern Arizona University. Mrs. Ford, as her students call her, has spent 20 years in the educational sector.

She uses her diverse background experience to build relationships and help people establish their own expectations in life. Lesley lives in Phoenix, Arizona with her husband and two loyal rottweilers.

Daughter. Wife. Friend. Teacher. Supporter.

9 781977 235633